ELLEN DEGENERES

Recent Titles in Greenwood Biographies

Sitting Bull: A Biography
Edward J. Rielly

Eleanor Roosevelt: A Biography
Cynthia M. Harris

Jesse Owens: A Biography
Jacqueline Edmondson

The Notorious B.I.G.: A Biography
Holly Lang

Hillary Clinton: A Biography
Dena B. Levy and Nicole R. Krassas

Johnny Depp: A Biography
Michael Blitz

Judy Blume: A Biography
Kathleen Tracy

Nelson Mandela: A Biography
Peter Limb

LeBron James: A Biography
Lew Freedman

Tecumseh: A Biography
Amy H. Sturgis

Diana, Princess of Wales: A Biography
Martin Gitlin

Nancy Pelosi: A Biography
Elaine S. Povich

Barack Obama: A Biography
JoAnn F. Price

ELLEN DEGENERES

A Biography

Lisa Iannucci

GREENWOOD BIOGRAPHIES

GREENWOOD PRESS
WESTPORT, CONNECTICUT • LONDON

Library of Congress Cataloging-in-Publication Data

Iannucci, Lisa.
    Ellen DeGeneres : a biography / Lisa Iannucci.
        p. cm. — (Greenwood biographies, ISSN 1540–4900)
    Includes bibliographical references and index.
    ISBN 978–0–313–35370–3 (alk. paper)
    1. DeGeneres, Ellen.   2. Comedians—United States—Biography.
3. Television personalities—United States—Biography.   I. Title.
    PN2287.D358 I26   2009
    792.702'8092—dc22
    [B]   2008030540

British Library Cataloguing in Publication Data is available.

Library of Congress Catalog Card Number: 2008030540

ISBN: 978–0–313–35370–3
ISSN: 1540–4900

First published in 2009

Greenwood Press, 88 Post Road West, Westport, CT 06881
An imprint of Greenwood Publishing Group, Inc.
www.greenwood.com

Printed in the United States of America

The paper used in this book complies with the
Permanent Paper Standard issued by the National
Information Standards Organization (Z39.48–1984).

10 9 8 7 6 5 4 3 2 1

CONTENTS

Series Foreword   vii

Foreword   ix

Acknowledgments   xi

Timeline: Events in the Life of Ellen DeGeneres   xiii

Chapter 1   The Birth of a Star   1

Chapter 2   Striking Out on Her Own   11

Chapter 3   A Funny Thing Happened…   25

Chapter 4   The Puppy Episode   35

Chapter 5   "Yep, I'm Gay"   43

Chapter 6   The Aftermath   51

Chapter 7   Bouncing Back   59

Chapter 8   Just Keep Dancing   77

Appendix: Awards   95

Bibliography   99

Index   103

Photo essay follows page 58

SERIES FOREWORD

In response to high school and public library needs, Greenwood developed this distinguished series of full-length biographies specifically for student use. Prepared by field experts and professionals, these engaging biographies are tailored for high school students who need challenging yet accessible biographies. Ideal for secondary school assignments, the length, format and subject areas are designed to meet educators' requirements and students' interests.

Greenwood offers an extensive selection of biographies spanning all curriculum-related subject areas including social studies, the sciences, literature and the arts, history and politics, as well as popular culture, covering public figures and famous personalities from all time periods and backgrounds, both historic and contemporary, who have made an impact on American and/or world culture. Greenwood biographies were chosen based on comprehensive feedback from librarians and educators. Consideration was given to both curriculum relevance and inherent interest. The result is an intriguing mix of the well known and the unexpected, the saints and sinners from long-ago history and contemporary pop culture. Readers will find a wide array of subject choices from fascinating crime figures like Al Capone to inspiring pioneers like Margaret Mead, from the greatest minds of our time like Stephen Hawking to the most amazing success stories of our day like J. K. Rowling.

While the emphasis is on fact, not glorification, the books are meant to be fun to read. Each volume provides in-depth information about the subject's life from birth through childhood, the teen years, and adulthood. A thorough account relates family background and education, traces personal and professional influences, and explores struggles, accomplishments, and contributions. A timeline highlights the most significant life events against a historical perspective. Bibliographies supplement the reference value of each volume.

FOREWORD

Ellen DeGeneres stood on the stage of her daytime talk show on February 29, 2008, urging viewers, "We must change our country, and we can do it. We can do it with our behavior; we can do it with the messages that we send our children. This is an election year and there's a lot of talk about change. I think one thing we should change is hate. Check out who you're voting for. Does that person really truly believe that we are all equal under the law? If you're not sure, I say change your vote. We deserve better."

It was a rare political move for a comic who has always, more than anything else, wanted to make people laugh. But just as Ellen edged out Oprah Winfrey for the top spot on the Harris Poll's annual list of America's favorite television stars,[1] the first openly gay person to ever do so, she took yet another risk by speaking openly and honestly about being gay in America.

I'll admit it. I have loved Ellen DeGeneres since I met her, pre-stardom, in a club in New Orleans in the 1980s. In the times I've spoken with her offscreen, I found her as warm, charming, funny, and sincere as she is on camera. She's funny and fascinating and remarkably savvy, but without the cynicism most celebrities hold so dear. She's also, hands down, one of the most important gay civil rights pioneers in the twentieth century.

No, she wasn't marching on Washington or getting bombed in Selma, Alabama, but Ellen took a series of personal risks and even more personal hits along the way, from saying "Yep, I'm Gay" on the cover of *Time* magazine to coming out to 42 million viewers on her sitcom to telling her now-massive daytime audience that February day about how America has failed to protect gay kids like recently murdered teenager Larry King.

Anyone who thinks a performer doesn't have the impact of a politician or preacher hasn't seen the so-called power of the pulpit that television, and all of Hollywood, has. Yet, Ellen has always used her capacity for influence and power for good, which has had a tremendous impact not just on the lesbian, gay, bisexual and transgender (LGBT) community, but on America at large. Who could forget her turn at the podium, come Emmy night, just after the 9/11 attacks: "What would upset the Taliban more than a gay woman wearing a suit in front of a room full of Jews?" she joked.

And though coming out on prime time and joining a media circus that would scrutinize everything from her poor box office to her high-profile romances to her penchant for Adidas sneakers and sensible pantsuits cost her a few years of happiness, it led the way for a pop-culture revolution that hasn't been seen in decades. Television shows as diverse as *Will & Grace, Two and a Half Men, Grey's Anatomy,* and *The L Word* have all found success thanks to her pioneering work.

Though she'll always be beloved by legions of women for her talk show, by legions of tweens for *Finding Nemo,* and by three generations of LGBT individuals for daring to be the first major star to come out on TV, no doubt the tremendous impact Ellen has had on our world as a funny woman with compassionate causes is just beginning to be understood.

Diane Anderson-Minshall
Executive Editor
Curve *magazine*

NOTE

1. http://www.harrisinteractive.com/harris_poll/index.asp?PID=858.

ACKNOWLEDGMENTS

I'd really like to thank the Gay and Lesbian Alliance Against Defamation (GLAAD) organization for supplying me with some great information. I would like to thank Patricia Quaglieri, my other researcher. I would also like to thank my editor, Kristi Ward of Greenwood Press, for some great suggestions and guidance along the way. I would also like to thank Ellen DeGeneres for reminding me of what I've believed during the years: that laughing, no matter what you're up against, can get you through anything. From the time I hummed the theme to *I Love Lucy* through contractions while giving birth to my third child to when I made sure to watch reruns of Abbott and Costello after I lost my husband, laughter has been really great medicine. It goes down easy and makes you feel good. Ellen is truly an inspiration.

TIMELINE: EVENTS IN THE LIFE OF ELLEN DEGENERES

January 26, 1958 Ellen DeGeneres is born at Ochsner Foundation Hospital in Jefferson, Louisiana—the second child to Betty and Elliott DeGeneres. Her only other sibling, brother Vance, was born two years earlier.

1971 Ellen's parents separate.

1973 Ellen's parents finalize their divorce.

1974 Ellen's mother remarries a man nicknamed "B" and is diagnosed with breast cancer.

1975 During her mother's recovery from a radical mastectomy, Ellen is molested by her stepfather.

June 1976 Graduates from Atlanta High School in Atlanta, Texas. Around this time, Ellen recognizes that she is attracted to women.

1980 Ellen's first serious girlfriend, 23-year-old Kat Perkoff, dies in a car accident. Ellen writes her legendary "Phone Call to God" skit.

1982 Ellen wins Showtime's "Funniest Person in Louisiana" contest and goes on to win the nationals; she is named "Funniest Person in America."

1985 Ellen comes in second place to comedian Sinbad in the San Francisco Comedy Festival.

1986   Performs at The Improv in Las Vegas, Nevada,
               and is spotted by a producer from *The Tonight
               Show Starring Johnny Carson*.
               Ellen films her first HBO Special, *Young Co-
               medians Reunion*.
January 1987   Ellen's debut on *The Tonight Show Starring
               Johnny Carson*. She is the first female comic
               to be called over to sit on Johnny's couch and
               talk with him.
1987 to 1989   Earns her first television role on Fox TV's sit-
               com *Open House* and gets good reviews; the
               sitcom is cancelled after only two seasons.
1991   Named "Best Female Standup" at the Ameri-
               can Comedy Awards.
1992   Appears on ABC's short-lived, six-episode sit-
               com *Laurie Hill*.
1993   Appears in the major motion picture *Cone-
               heads*, based on the *Saturday Night Live* skit.
March 29, 1994 Debuts her television sitcom *These Friends of
               Mine*. Reviews are great, and the show returns
               later that fall renamed *Ellen*.
September   Co-hosts the Primetime Emmy Awards to rave
               reviews.
1995   Publishes her first humorous book, *My Point . . .
               and I Do Have One*. The book makes the *New
               York Times* bestseller list.
September 24, 1996   Rumors fly that her sitcom character, Ellen
               Morgan, will announce she's a lesbian and
               that Ellen DeGeneres will announce her own
               homosexuality as well. Gay and Lesbian Alli-
               ance Against Defamation (GLAAD) launches
               its "Let Ellen Out!" campaign and develops
               Ellen Watch, a Web page dedicated to moni-
               toring the show and following the title charac-
               ter's journey in coming out.
April 14, 1997 Ellen appears on the cover of *Time* magazine
               with the headline, "Yep, I'm Gay."

Begins relationship with actress Anne Heche, whom she brings to the White House Correspondents' Dinner where she takes pictures with President Bill Clinton.

April 30 Ellen Morgan's coming out. "The Puppy Episode" is shown, and more than 42 million people tune in. GLAAD coordinated "Come Out With Ellen" house parties in more than 1,500 households nationwide. An ABC affiliate in Birmingham, Alabama, refuses to air the episode. GLAAD organizes a satellite-fed telecast of the episode attended by 3,000 people.

Ellen's mother is asked to become the Human Rights Campaign's (HRC) National Coming Out spokesperson.

December Named "Entertainer of the Year" by *Entertainment Weekly*.

April 1998 Ellen is honored at the 9th Annual GLAAD Media Awards with the Stephen F. Kolzak Award, presented to an openly LGBT media professional who has made a significant difference in promoting equal rights for the community.

April 23 Last episode of *Ellen*—the show is cancelled.

1999 Ellen's mother, Betty DeGeneres, authors *Love, Ellen: A Mother/Daughter Journey*.

Ellen appears in the romantic comedy *The Love Letter*, with Tom Selleck.

Ellen is cast as Sergeant Rita Pompano in the 1999 *Goodbye Lover*, costarring Don Johnson, Dermot Mulroney, and Mary-Louise Parker.

July 2000 Ellen's first HBO Comedy Special, *Ellen DeGeneres: The Beginning*, which is nominated for two Emmy Awards.

September 24, 2001 Ellen's new sitcom, *The Ellen Show*, premieres on CBS but is cancelled after only 13 episodes.

November Ellen hosts the 53rd Annual Primetime Emmy Awards.

September 8, 2003   Ellen launches her daytime talk show, *The Ellen DeGeneres Show*. The show wins multiple Daytime Emmy Awards over the next few years.

2004   Ellen is chosen as the first openly gay person to represent American Express in its new "My life. My card." campaign.

January 2005   Ellen is on the cover of *The Advocate*, photographed by partner Alexandra Hedison. Their relationship ends before the issue hits the stands, and Ellen starts dating actress Portia de Rossi.

April 2006   Ellen wins her second Daytime Emmy for Outstanding Talk Show Host.

February 25, 2007   Ellen hosts the Academy Awards.

April 30   The Oxygen network re-airs "The Puppy Episode" to celebrate the episode's 10th anniversary, 10 years to the day it originally aired on ABC.

May 15, 2008   California allows same-sex marriages. On her talk show, Ellen announces that she and Portia intend to marry later in the year.

August 16, 2008   Ellen married her girlfriend Portia de Rossi at their home in Beverly Hills, California.

Chapter 1

THE BIRTH OF A STAR

People always ask me, Were you funny as a child? Well, no, I was
an accountant.

—*Ellen DeGeneres*

In January 2008, Ellen sat in a maroon armchair on the set of her
Emmy Award–winning daily talk show *Ellen*, faced the cameras, and
addressed her studio audience about a serious topic in her life—her
50th birthday. The birthday girl, who premiered her talk show in
September 2003, just wanted one present, and it had to do with
Brad Pitt.

Although many women in her studio audience would instantly say
that Brad Pitt *is* the ultimate birthday present and stop there, that's
not what Ellen had in mind on this celebratory day. For her special
occasion, the normally humorous, award-winning comedian—who
regularly dances over tables, plays video games on national TV,
blogs about her variety of lunches, and when injured continues to
host her talk show from a mobile hospital bed—was totally serious.
All she asked for was help—she wanted her home and studio audiences to contribute to the efforts of actor and humanitarian Brad
Pitt to rebuild New Orleans, an area still reeling from the devastating effects of Hurricane Katrina, one of the most deadly hurricanes
in U.S. history, which struck on August 29, 2005.

Katrina's vicious storm and the accompanying powerful water
surge damaged the Gulf Coast and devastated many Mississippi cities.

In Louisiana, the federal flood protection system in New Orleans failed, and nearly every levee in metro New Orleans breached, flooding 80 percent of the city and many areas of neighboring parishes for weeks. Through Pitt's Make It Right NOLA Foundation, 150 affordable and sustainable homes would be created. Members of Team Ellen became foster parents to one such home, and Ellen's fan base worldwide contributed donations to be used to purchase furnishings, appliances, and more for the victims of Hurricane Katrina in Louisiana.

It was in Pass Christian, Mississippi, that Ellen's 82-year-old Aunt Currie lost everything to Hurricane Katrina. "Pass Christian...is just gone. There's not one building left—no church, no nothing," said Ellen. And it was in Louisiana where Ellen Lee DeGeneres was born. Fifty years later, she was giving back to the community that she loved so much.[1]

Ellen made her way into the world on January 26, 1958, at Ochsner Foundation Hospital in Jefferson, Louisiana. Jefferson is located on the East Bank of the Mississippi River and is part of the Greater New Orleans Metropolitan area. In the book *Love, Ellen: A Mother/Daughter Journey*, published in 1999, Ellen's mother, Betty DeGeneres, remembers when she was pregnant with Ellen, a pregnancy that she says she had to fight for because of her husband's reluctance to have more children. "Ellen was indeed a miracle," she writes. "I had to beg for a second child. Elliott thought one child, whom we dearly loved, was sufficient. Nothing if not tenacious, I didn't give up. I thank God every day that I persevered and so does Elliott."[2]

The mother of Ellen DeGeneres was born Betty Pfeffer in 1930 in New Orleans, the birthplace of jazz. She was the youngest of three girls to William and Mildred Pfeffer. She grew up in the area, attending Louisiana State University in Baton Rouge. It was when she was at college that she met her first husband, a 21-year-old whom she would marry when she was 19 years old. The marriage only lasted a year. A few years later, in 1952, she would marry Elliott DeGeneres in a Methodist church, a man she knew casually through the Christian Science Young Peoples Social Group and reconnected with later when she was job searching. The couple celebrated the birth of their 9-pound 13-ounce baby daughter, whom Betty called "a beautiful blob of fatness." Ellen became the second child of

Elliott and Betty, with her older brother, Vance, born four years earlier on September 2, 1954. Elliott supported the family in his job as an insurance salesman. Betty would hold a variety of jobs—from employment counselor to speech pathologist.

Ellen was a typical child—she played with her older brother Vance and played outside until after dark with the neighborhood children. She loved animals and idolized famed zoologist Dian Fossey, who studied gorillas for years in the Rwanda mountain forests. Like many kids dreaming about what they wanted to be when they grew up, Ellen daydreamed about leaving New Orleans to become a naturalist—an expert in natural history—or joining the Peace Corps to study apes in Africa just like Fossey.

It was the 1960s and young Ellen had a typical childhood, enjoying riding her bike, being a tomboy, wearing frilly dresses, and playing with dolls and babies. She also enjoyed watching television shows and listening to music. It was an era that musical legends were made of, including the Beatles, the Beach Boys, Motown, the Rolling Stones, and, of course, the renowned Elvis Presley. Black-and-white television shows reflected old-fashioned ideas of family values—there were the favorites such as *Ozzie and Harriet, Father Knows Best, The Danny Thomas Show,* and the *Andy Griffith Show.* Families would gather around the television set while eating dinner for special quality time. Ellen's favorites were *The Ed Sullivan Show, The Dick Van Dyke Show,* and *I Love Lucy.* Ellen also enjoyed watching such comic greats as Jack Benny, who had his own show from the 1950s through the mid-1960s and was known for his exasperated "Well!" Ellen also idolized famed 1950s comedian George Gobel and the comedy team of Bob and Ray who had their own show in the 1950s. Ellen's attraction to watching all types of comedy was perhaps an unknowing early training for her future career and a sign of what was to come.

It was an exciting time to be a child growing up in New Orleans, too. The era was considered a decade of transformation, with the battle for civil rights, desegregation, and the creation of their first professional sports franchise—the New Orleans Saints—and the Superdome. Unfortunately, the 1960s also brought a significant and tragic hurricane—Hurricane Betsy arrived with a vengeance in 1965, and the Industrial Canal breached and flooded the lower ninth ward as well as nearby towns. The 1960s were known as a time of sex, drugs, and rock and roll (the legendary Woodstock concert event was held in 1969). The 1960s was about experimentation in all of these areas, and people expressed their desire to be free.

Ellen's parents, however, weren't following this sexual revolution. Instead, they were two devoutly religious Christian Scientists, members of the Church of Christ, Scientist, which was created by Mary Baker Eddy almost 140 years ago in the United States.[3] Eddy was a devoted student of the Bible, which is foundational to the practice of Christian Science. Christian Scientists also believe that the first choice for healing illness is prayer, although there is no biblical or church mandate to forgo medical intervention. Christian Scientists also do not believe that heaven or hell are places in an afterlife, instead they are a state of mind. Betty's introduction to Christian Scientists began when her mother wanted to use birth control after the birth of her three children but was told it was forbidden by her church, the Catholic Church. As a result, Betty's mom turned to the Christian Scientists for spiritual support, although she never officially joined the church. She raised her children as Christian Scientists.

Elliott was also a firm believer in Christian Science, but this spiritual connection would not make the marriage a solid one. Betty described her "shell of a marriage" that, to the outsider looking in, could really have been mistaken for the perfect television family, such as in the classic television show *Ozzie and Harriet*, except with one boy and one girl. In these television shows, everybody always seemed happy, problems were small, and they were handled by talking things out. But to Betty, the lack of communication between her and Elliott, and his vastly different ideas about having children, made her marriage far from the idealized family and marriage that was portrayed on television.[4]

Even in a 1997 interview with Diane Sawyer, when reflecting on his childhood, Vance said, "The DeGeneres' just were not big talkers in the house. You didn't talk about things." Betty, eager to explain that it was only for the unpleasant items, was corrected by Vance, who said, "Well, even if it was pleasant."[5] The marriage hit a pivotal rock bottom when Betty left the Christian Scientists and became intrigued by the Episcopal Church, which seemed to offer her a sense of ritual that the Christian Scientists didn't have.

After grasping that the marriage would never be what Betty needed and would be hindered by Elliott's devotion to Christian Science, Betty took what she saw as a huge risk and left her husband in 1971 when Ellen was 13 years old. The decision is one she says she later regretted, and that if Elliot had only fought for her to stay, she might have changed her mind.[6] Anxious to move on, yet still mourning her failed relationship, Betty packed up and rented an apartment with Vance and Ellen. The couple's divorce was final in 1973.

For the teenaged Ellen, this was an arduous time, but it was also a time in which Ellen discovered the benefits of comedy. She used it time and again to help her mother laugh when she was blue. "My mother was going through some really hard times and I could see when she was really getting down, and I would start to make fun of her dancing," DeGeneres remembered. "Then she'd start to laugh and I'd make fun of her laughing. And she'd laugh so hard she'd start to cry, and then I'd make fun of that. So I would totally bring her from where I'd seen her start going into depression to all the way out of it."[7]

Ellen did what many comic greats have done in their youth—used humor help get through difficult situations in their life. For example, Jim Carrey, whose family was homeless when his father, Percy, lost his job, would make the family laugh—and ultimately financially support them—by doing impersonations of relatives and celebrities. Chris Rock used comedy to keep from getting beat up by bullies, which later became the premise of his sitcom *Everybody Hates Chris*. Little did Ellen know at this point in her young life that her ability to use comedy to help cope with tremendously challenging situations would be pivotal later in her career. First, during the trials and tribulations of making it as a stand-up comic and later during her memorable meeting with the legendary talk-show host Johnny Carson.

Betty and Elliott's divorce came at a time when Ellen was just beginning her vulnerable teenage years—a time when young adults are anxious to fit in among their peers. Ellen loved her friends and her hometown of Metairie and New Orleans, where as a child she spent much of her free time exploring on her bike. "I rode my bike everywhere. All over the campus [of Newcomb College]. All over uptown. You know, people can grow up in New Orleans without realizing how unique a city it is," she told Liz Scott of *New Orleans Magazine*.

But Ellen's comfort zone would soon be drastically altered when her mom decided to start dating again two years later. Like many divorced women, Betty was fearful of the dating scene. However, once she took the plunge, she cherished the attention, especially from one particular man, whom for this book we will call "B." (Editorial note: B is mentioned by name in other books, but not in Betty's biography. For this book we have chosen to respect Ellen and Betty and not mention him by name.) B, a cowboy-type whom Betty met at her apartment building, was unlike Elliott in every way—he was less spiritual, more macho, and a man who seemed to easily charm Betty.[8] As a result, she embarked on a whirlwind romance with the salesman and married him in 1974.

In the 1970s and early 1980s, an area of bars and nightclubs opened in a section of Metairie known as "Fat City." Today, Metairie even has its own so-called family-friendly version of the famous New Orleans Mardi Gras. But it was back then during the "Fat City" years that 16-year-old Ellen started to do what many teens do—she became more rebellious, hanging out late at night with the older crowd from her Grace King High School and drinking beer.

Betty wanted to remove Ellen from the negative influences and start over with her new husband in a new area, so when B got a new sales job in the small town of Atlanta, Texas (population 6,400 in 2008), she relocated with Ellen. Atlanta is located 20 miles south of Texarkana and more than 400 miles away from Ellen's former New Orleans home. The small town was named after Atlanta, Georgia. There was a small downtown area consisting of a few stores and many churches, and visitors would come to fish and hunt in the various lakes and streams. While B worked his sales job, Betty worked in various secretarial positions.

Ellen called Atlanta a "confining atmosphere," but she did exactly what Betty had hoped—she fit in during her high school years, played tennis, and became quite popular—and none of that beer-drinking business. Ellen even had a steady boyfriend at the time, Ben Heath.[9] Meanwhile, her big brother, Vance, was coming into his own as an aspiring 17-year-old musician and singer who played guitar in the junior high band, the Dark Ages. Following high school graduation, he hit the road to start his own music career. His first gig was at a party for a neighborhood kid where he was supposed to be paid a nominal fee of $10. Instead, the children threw cookies, but it didn't deter Vance from his musical dreams.

Ellen had a close relationship with Vance. She looked up to him and yet was eager for the same attention he was receiving from his own audiences and fans: "I wanted to have money, I wanted to be special. I wanted people to like me. I wanted to be famous. When you're growing up and see your brother who's talented and gorgeous and all these things, you want to be all those things. I thought if I could find a way to be famous, people would love me."[10]

To an outsider, the DeGeneres family looked more and more like the perfect family—with Betty's new marriage and two happy, successful children. Unfortunately—and eerily similar to other previous family experiences—things still weren't as they seemed. Behind closed doors, B was considered bossy, crude, and insensitive, and teenaged Ellen just didn't like him. And to top it all off, several traumatic events were about to happen to both mother and daughter that would change their lives forever.

THE UNTHINKABLE

In 1975, there were no pink awareness ribbons, no monthly breast examinations, no Susan G. Komen Foundation, and no talk about cancer, especially not about breast cancer. So when Betty felt a lump in her breast during a routine physical examination, she was scared, although for Ellen she tried to remain strong and confident that she would be okay. She reassured the then 16-year-old that the routine biopsy procedure that she had to undergo was nothing to be concerned about and that she would return home quickly.

However, that wasn't to be the case. What was to be a standard biopsy turned into a modified radical mastectomy—the only treatment available to women at that time, no matter what stage of cancer they were in. According to BreastCancer.org, a modified radical mastectomy removes the entire breast and includes a procedure called axillary dissection, in which two of three levels of the lymph nodes in the underarm area are removed.

"Everything was a dirty little secret back then," said Ellen. "The fact that she had a mastectomy was not spoken of. She tried to shield me from it a little bit, but she needed my help with recovery and physical rehabilitation. It bonded us even more."[11]

So while her mother was being treated for breast cancer, Ellen, a dedicated daughter who obviously loved her mother very much, remained by her side and tended to her every need during treatment and physical therapy. However, what her mother didn't know was that Ellen was enduring her own personal crisis. It was during this onerous time, this tender recovery from Betty's life-threatening disease, that Ellen says B molested her. Dedicated to her mother's recovery, Ellen was afraid that telling her would deter Betty's recovery, so Ellen kept it a secret.[12] At this point, keeping a secret didn't seem to be a difficult thing to do in a family that wasn't very garrulous to begin with.

According to Ellen's recounting of the events, B told her that "he thinks he feels a lump in (my mother's) other breast, but he doesn't want to alarm her so he needs to feel mine to make sure." B made her lie down "because he said he felt hers while she was lying down," she tells *Allure*.[13] Ellen also explained that this groping led to "other things" including an episode where he attempted to break into her bedroom at a time when Ellen says her grandmother was dying, too. Ellen kicked out a window and escaped to a friend's home for the night.[14]

Reflecting on her childhood, Ellen once confessed she was fearful growing up. When asked what she was fearful of, Ellen replied, "Afraid of anything; my experience was denial about real feelings, denial about pure joy and crazy, screaming happiness. There was no anger and screaming lows. But I'm really grateful for everything that I went through because (I decided) this is what I had to overcome; I was going to take chances. I was going to be different. I was going to be successful. I was going to have money."[15]

Ellen needed to flee from her stepfather's abuse. The legendary crooner Tony Bennett sang about leaving his heart in San Francisco, but to Ellen, it was Louisiana that was pulling at her heartstrings, and it was the place she always called home. So once she knew her mother had recovered and after her 1976 graduation from Atlanta High School in Atlanta, Texas, Ellen immediately moved back in with her father, stepmother, and her stepmother's two children in Louisiana. It was time to concentrate on her own future.

NOTES

1. http://www.foxnews.com/printer_friendly_story/0,3566,168206,00.html.

2. Betty DeGeneres, *Love, Ellen: A Mother/Daughter Journey* (New York: William Morrow & Co., 1999), p. 69.

3. http://www.tfccs.com/media/faq.jhtml.

4. Betty DeGeneres, *Love, Ellen*, p. 102.

5. http://www.ellen-forum.de/ellen/presse/sawyer1.html.

6. Betty DeGeneres, *Love, Ellen*, p. 86.

7. http://www.notablebiographies.com/news/Ca-Ge/DeGeneres-Ellen.html)—format.

8. Betty DeGeneres, *Love, Ellen*, p. 109.

9. Kathleen Tracy, *Ellen: The Real Story of Ellen DeGeneres* (New York: Pinnacle, 2005), p. 31.

10. www.style.com/w/feat_story/020707/full_page.html.

11. http://www.people.com/people/article/0,,20058779,00.html.

12. http://www.cbsnews.com/stories/2005/05/18/entertainment/main696352.shtml.

13. *Allure*, June 2005, p. 194.

14. http://www.people.com/people/article/0,,1062732,00.html.

15. http://www.tv.com/ellen-degeneres/person/20796/trivia.html.

Chapter 2

STRIKING OUT ON HER OWN

My grandmother started walking five miles a day when she was sixty.
She's ninety-seven now, and we don't know where the hell she is.

—*Ellen DeGeneres*

Like many high school graduates, the next natural progression for
Ellen after relocating back to Louisiana was to enroll in college
and work on obtaining her college degree. Ellen enrolled at the
University of New Orleans—which is often called UNO by local
residents—to major in communications. However, matriculating
was not to be in the comedian's future, and she dropped out after
only one semester.

At the same time that Ellen was searching for a career, she was
holding on to another secret—a secret about her sexuality that she
had yet to tell her parents and one she had only come to accept
for herself during this time. The young blonde-haired, blue-eyed
Ellen was popular in high school and had a few boyfriends, including Ricky Partain, who even gave Ellen a promise ring but said later
in an interview that if she lost the token of his affection, it wasn't
worth much.

In her heart, Ellen felt different compared to the other boy-crazy
teenaged girls. She was a self-confessed tomboy, and although she
liked men, she was never really attracted to them. Thinking she was
just a late bloomer and proud of herself for being a virgin, Ellen was
still conflicted emotionally because when it came to sexuality, she

knew that she was attracted to women. She didn't quite know what to do with these feelings. While she knew she was gay, she didn't feel that she was part of either the gay or straight communities. In two different interviews, Ellen provided an introspective of how she felt at that tender teenage time in her life:

> No. I ignored it because I didn't really know what it was until I was 18 years old. I dated guys. I liked guys. But I knew that I liked girls too. I just didn't know what to do with that. I thought, "If I were a guy I'd go out with her." And then I thought, "Well, I don't want to be a guy, really." So I went, "Oh, well," and just went on with my life. My first gay experience was literally someone else's idea—I was freaked out even by the thought of it. And I thought that was one experience and it was just her, and I started dating guys again, thinking, "Well, I just need to meet the right one." Never could, really.[1]

Ellen accepted her own sexual orientation and began lesbian relationships, but she still needed to share this news with her family. It was important to find the right opportunity to tell them. For her mom, Ellen chose to tell her during a walk on the beach in Pass Christian, Mississippi in 1977, when on a family vacation she finally said the words, "Mom, I'm gay." According to Betty, the then 19-year-old Ellen, who was blossoming into an independent young adult, also told her, "Mom, I'm in love. It's with a woman." Ellen sobbed, but those weren't tears of fear. Ellen was relieved that her news was out in the open. While many gays and lesbians find it difficult to tell their parents about their homosexuality, Ellen admitted in interviews later in her career that she didn't see this as a difficult thing to do. Betty hugged her daughter, but, at the same time, this sympathetic mom felt helpless and scared.

Although Betty supported Ellen, Betty was raised in the 1930s and 1940s, when women were taught to marry and depend on a man for financial and emotional security. Things back then were much different than they were in the 1960s, when Betty was raising Ellen. But as a gay woman, Ellen still had to face a different world—one that wasn't necessarily accepting of her sexual orientation. In addition, Betty considered herself a stranger to this lifestyle and was still worried about who would take care of her daughter financially, since a man wouldn't be in the picture. In an interview with Diane Sawyer, Betty said that until that very moment on the beach she had not even suspected that Ellen was gay, because of the fact that she had boyfriends in high school. When Sawyer asked Betty if she was horrified that her daughter was gay, Betty replied, "No, I wasn't horrified. Worried. Worried."[2]

Regardless of how Betty might have felt about her daughter's sexual orientation, she would always support her. This is often not the case for many parents who find out that their child is gay, and Betty's support was especially rare for the time period. In the 1950s, consensual gay sex was still considered a felony with possible prison sentences of up to 20 years. In the 1960s, there was a sexual revolution, but the gay community was still shunned and often tormented. In the late 1960s, the lesbian, gay, bisexual, transsexual (LGBT) community was repeatedly harassed with multiple raids on gay bars followed by numerous arrests. In June 1969, the New York City gay community fought back for their rights—literally. After several raids on gay bars in the area over a period of time, New York City police raided the Stonewall Inn gay bar in Greenwich Village and arrested employees and drag performers. However, more than 2,000 lesbian, gay, and transgender supporters resisted arrest, inciting riots and calls for equal gay rights from gay leaders. Gay pride parades and marches were organized in Los Angeles, San Francisco, and Chicago and were held yearly after that, including in 1979 when more than 100,000 gays and lesbians marched on Washington. The Stonewall Riots were considered the start of the gay liberation movement.

In the 1970s, although the television industry started to make some strides by adding gay supporting characters or gay story lines to their sitcoms, being gay on a television sitcom was not exactly the same as being gay in real life. Outside of Hollywood, being gay and lesbian was considered a mental health disorder by the psychiatric community, and gays were still fighting for the same basic rights that heterosexuals had—the right to marry and the right to adopt children.

After the Stonewall Riots, gays and lesbians began to fight for their right to come "out of the closet" and into mainstream America. Organizations were founded on behalf of the gay community to promote equality and acceptance. In 1972, the Parents, Families and Friends of Lesbians and Gays (PFLAG) was founded by Jeanne Manford after she marched with her son, Mortie, in New York City's Gay Pride Parade. Two months earlier, her son was beaten at a gay rights protest while police did nothing.

In 1973, the National Gay Task Force Foundation was founded in New York and worked to change the American Psychiatric Association's classification of homosexuality as a mental disorder. In 1980, the Human Rights Campaign was founded to raise money for congressional candidates who supported fairness to LGBT Americans. In the years that followed, the organization established itself as a resilient force in the overall movement for gay, lesbian, bisexual, and transgender civil rights as it strived to achieve fundamental fairness and equality for all. In 1985, the Gay and Lesbian Alliance Against Defamation (GLAAD) was formed in New York to protest the *New York Post's* grossly defamatory and sensationalized AIDS coverage. Once the organization got underway, its work expanded to Los Angeles, where it educated Hollywood's entertainment industry on the importance of more accurate and realistic portrayals on the screen. There were also gay rights protests and marches, but it didn't mean that homosexuality was more accepted in mainstream American society. Hate crimes were a common occurrence.

However, at Ellen's home, her mother wasn't embarrassed by her daughter. Betty wasn't the type of parent who blamed herself as if Ellen's homosexuality was an error in parenting. Instead, Betty did everything she could to learn about the homosexual lifestyle and how to embrace her daughter for who she was. "In time, I would come to appreciate and admire her for not being like everyone else and for her strength, courage and honesty in being exactly who she was supposed to be," writes Betty in *Love, Ellen*.[3] In time, Betty would also become an advocate for rights for the gay community.

Ellen's older brother, Vance, who loved his sister and supported her, took the news that his sister was gay in stride, served up with a side dish of humor, a coping tool in the DeGeneres family. Upon hearing the news, Vance joked with Ellen that they probably had even dated the same women at one time. Unfortunately, her father's reaction was not what Ellen had hoped it would be. Elliott kicked Ellen out of the home he then shared with his new wife and stepchildren, concerned that Ellen's lifestyle would influence his stepchildren. However, he did help Ellen to get an apartment and admitted later to Diane Sawyer that kicking her out was a mistake.[4]

For the next few years—and what seemed like potential fodder for future comedy skits—Ellen held down many jobs in the New Orleans area. She sold clothes at the Merry-Go-Round chain store at the Lakeside Shopping Center, served food, painted houses, worked at a car wash, bartended, wrapped gifts (this job actually did turn into part of her stand-up comedy routines), sold Hoover vacuums, and shucked oysters. As Ellen says, "When you live in New Orleans, you're bound to be an oyster shucker, aren't ya?"[5]

Similar to her college experience, though, Ellen realized that these various odd jobs were not going to give her a future. The good news was that she finally realized where that future was—Ellen wanted to make people laugh. Like many aspiring comedians, Ellen knew that she had to start her career by performing in smaller venues and working her way up, so when a friend asked her to perform at a luncheon, she obliged. Ellen gained some exposure and experience and continued to perform at small clubs and coffeehouses in New Orleans as well as college venues.

Unlike other famous stand-up comedians of the time—such as Richard Pryor, Robin Williams, or Eddie Murphy—Ellen's material was free of vulgarity and put-downs. There were no discriminatory jokes of any kind. Instead, Ellen took everyday occurrences that she experienced and related them to her audience.

Describing her own brand of humor, she says, "I don't know that I can ever get perspective on who I am to other people. I know who I am and how I feel inside, and I know that it's kind. It's not mean-spirited humor—it's not a joke at someone else's expense. I've never been interested in that. So I know that it's nice humor, and sometimes it's silly, and sometimes it's smart, but other than that I don't know how to label it."[6] For example, during one of her first gigs, her whole act involved eating a Burger King Whopper and fries. The gist of the skit was how someone would take a bite of food, try to speak, have you wait a minute while they finished, but then take yet another bite. The joke was a hit, and Ellen found herself getting paid to make people laugh, even if it was only a pittance. She knew that she had to write more material, though. "I knew instinctively I couldn't just keep eating onstage," said Ellen in an interview for the *New York Times*. "Oh, hey, it's that girl who eats on stage. Gee, she's huge!"[7] To keep her material fresh, Ellen regularly wrote new jokes and changed her style along the way, from the use of props in her early standup to the use of stories and words in her later sets.

Life was looking up for the 21-year-old. Her comedy career was on the rise; her mother had accepted her homosexuality, and Ellen was more comfortable in her own skin. At this time, Ellen was also in the throes of a serious relationship with 23-year-old poet Kat Perkoff, who ran a lesbian bar in the French Quarter of New Orleans. Perkoff's sister, Rachel, told *People* magazine that the two were very creative people who were young, crazy, and very much in love.[8]

Ellen was happy and that translated into new funny material for her routines. Unfortunately, this relationship wasn't without its problems. Ellen discovered the heartbreaking truth that Kat had cheated on her. Ellen left to "teach Kat a lesson" but had every intention of returning. Sadly, Ellen would never get the chance. In the summer of 1980, Kat died in a terrible car accident. "[Sighs] I had seen her right before the accident too," Ellen said. "The most horrible part of it was, she was cheating on me and we were living together. I moved out to teach her a lesson, thinking that I'd go back. So I was staying with someone else at the time. My brother's band was performing that night, and I saw her at the club. It was really loud, and she kept saying, 'When are you going to come home?' And I kept acting like I couldn't hear her, like the music was too loud. She left first, and then I left. We drove past the accident she was in."[9]

Ellen mourned Kat's death, yet at the same time she forged ahead and continued her burgeoning career. However, things weren't going so well. Since Ellen roomed with Kat—even though she had moved out temporarily—this tragedy left her without a girlfriend and a roommate. As a result, Ellen moved out of the apartment into a flea-infested rundown dwelling. Like many who cope with such a terrible loss, Ellen tried to make sense of it all. One day, she says, she tried to turn to God for the answers and wanted to know why a precious life like Kat's was tragically cut short while the fleas that infested her apartment, and seemingly had no other purpose but to annoy her while she tried to cope with life's twists and turns, were allowed to live on. Desperate for a response, Ellen tapped into her imagination and concocted what she thought God would say to her in a pretend phone conversation between the two: "No, I didn't realize how many people were employed by the flea collar industry. No, I didn't realize that thousands of people would be put out of work at the flea circus."[10]

The side-splitting make-believe dialogue that erupted inside Ellen's grief-stricken mind became known as her legendary "Phone Call to God" skit. She wrote the parody for what seemed to be self-therapeutic purposes and did not know that this sketch would catapult her comedy career to new heights, although she says she did visualize it.

"I'm sitting on this mattress infested with fleas [in 1980], and I thought, 'I'm going to do this on Johnny Carson, and I'm going to get called over to the couch, and I'll be the first woman in history ever to get called over,'" she said on *Today*. "I had created that experience because I wanted it."[11] In the meantime, while Ellen hoped for her Johnny Carson couch daydream to come true, she scored a gig at Clyde's Comedy Corner in the French Quarter of New Orleans where she gained more visibility and a regular gig, doing one show a night during the week and two shows on the weekends. Ellen's pittance became $300 a week. She soon worked her way up the comedic ladder at the Comedy Corner from performing 10-minute skits to 45-minute performances. She performed there for more than a year when she took second place in Clyde's amateur comedy competition. As a result of this victory, she was promoted to the club's emcee.

It was in the 1980s when stand-up comedy programs became popular on many cable televisions stations, such as HBO and Showtime. In 1982, Showtime held their "Funniest Person in Louisiana" contest. Ellen entered, won, and moved on to compete in the finals for Showtime's "Funniest Person in America."

She captured that crown as well. As part of her victory package, Ellen hosted Showtime specials and toured cities in a Winnebago being billed as "America's Funniest Person." This might sound like a great title, but, according to Robert Weider of the *San Francisco Chronicle*, "veteran comics wondered whether to marvel or spit."[12] Ellen loved the experience, but with the win came the responsibility of headlining the club. At the same time, she endured a lot of criticism since she had been advertised and billed as the funniest comedian. Ellen also told the *New York Times* that there was unwarranted competition between her and the other stand-up comics because of this title. "All the people working in the club would get on stage and try to blow me away because they were angry and bitter that I didn't have the experience, and here I was surpassing them," she said.[13]

The jealousy, mean-spiritedness, and competition temporarily dampened Ellen's spirits—she even called her mother and told her she wanted to get out of the business—but she toughed it out and didn't back down. Instead, she knew that in order to succeed in the cutthroat business of comedy, she would need to keep getting stronger. For an up-and-coming comedian looking to break into the big time though, she needed an agent, better bookings, and to perform in one of two places: New York or California. Although other cities hosted comedy venues and events, it was mostly in Los Angeles and New York City that comics found showcase clubs like the Improv, Caroline's, and The Laugh Factory. Young comedians performed at these venues hoping to be seen regularly and optimistic that an agent, scout, or other executive would notice their talents and move them on to even bigger and better appearances. It was Ellen's Showtime victory that finally influenced her to take her career to the next level—move to California and shoot for the big time.

BIG BROTHER AND MR. BILL

While Ellen started to carve out a place in show business, big brother Vance was succeeding as an entertainer in his own right. He served a two-year stint in the Marines because he thought he needed some discipline, and he finished his tour as a corporal.

In the early 1970s, Vance hosted a radio program called *New Wave New Orleans* broadcast on the WRNO station, known today as 995FM. Vance also played bass guitar with several New Orleans bands, including The Cold, at Jimmy's Music Club in uptown New Orleans. The Cold was a new-wave band with a self-described style of music similar to the rock band Blondie, led by platinum-blonde recording artist Deborah Harry, the punk/new-wave band the Rezillos, the Beatles, and the Dave Clark Five. The group went on to split up twice within a few short years and then returned for several reunion performances in the 1980s.

Ellen wasn't the only DeGeneres family member to have a sense of humor; Vance loved comedy and proved that he was quite good at it. When he was 18 years old, he and a friend, Wally Williams, performed impromptu skits at parties—what he calls "Bob & Ray type stuff." Bob Elliott and Ray Goulding were legendary humorists, considered pioneers in their field. Vance also listened to Wood Allen; Richard Pryor, The Firesign Theatre, which was a comedy troupe with Phil Austin; Peter Bergman; David Ossman; and Philip Proctor.[14]

Inspired by their comedy icons, the friends shot short comedy films that were shown in venues around the New Orleans area. These films became known as *The Mr. Bill Show* and followed the dangerous escapades of Mr. Bill, a clay figurine; his friend, Spot the dog; the mean Mr. Sluggo; Mr. Hands, played by Vance; and several other characters. In a great twist of fate, one Mr. Bill episode was ultimately shown on the hit NBC variety show *Saturday Night Live*. This one appearance triggered a successful four-year run for the pair from 1976 to 1980. Mr. Bill's signature exasperated phrase "Oh nooooo!" also became a pop-culture phenomenon. Unfortunately, Williams and Vance had a falling out in the early 1980s over ownership of Mr. Bill and later ended up in court determining how to split the profits made from the character.

Music pulled at Vance once again, and he couldn't stay away from the gigs, so he formed yet another band, called the House of Schock, with future Go-Go's drummer Gina Schock. The band recorded their only album, the self-titled *House of Schock*, in 1988 and was signed by Capitol Records. Unfortunately, the album was not promoted properly and was considered a failure. The talented artist Vance, however, was considered a standout by critics. Schock and Vance cowrote some songs that appeared in the major motion pictures *Bull Durham* and *The Accused*.

CALIFORNIA HERE I COME

Back in Louisiana in 1986, the DeGeneres matriarch was going through a rough period, what would now be called empty nest syndrome. Ellen and Vance were slowly building lives of their own in the world, and this gave Betty the time to examine her relationship with B. After moving with him from New Orleans to Tyler, Texas, Betty realized that it was time to file for a separation and take control of her life. Intent on pursuing a career that would have a positive impact on others, she headed back to New Orleans and enrolled in Louisiana State University, Shreveport, where she earned a master's degree in communication disorders. Betty later went on to become a speech pathologist for the New Orleans school system.

Betty graduated at the end of 1986, and after two rounds of leaving B and returning home and moving in with her ailing mother, Betty made the final move to end the marriage. She packed up and relocated to California to be closer to her children. Vance was on the road and ready to play in a new band, and Ellen was on her way to the Golden State to try and make it as a stand up comedian. Ellen set up residence in San Francisco and hit the area venues, even finishing second at the San Francisco Comedy Festival in 1985 (she was edged out by the comedian Sinbad).

When Ellen was trying to burst onto the California scene, stand-up comedy was not an innovative form of entertainment. Comedic monologues can be traced as far back as the golden age of radio, to such greats as Bob Hope and Jack Benny. Through the years, new talents would emerge, including satirist Lenny Bruce, Phyllis Diller, Redd Foxx, Freddy Prinze, Lily Tomlin, George Carlin, Rodney Dangerfield, and Steve Martin. In the 1980s, stand-up comedy was becoming more and more popular, and such stars as Robin Williams, Billy Crystal, and Eddie Murphy were fast becoming celebrities in the comedy venues, on television, and in the movies.

However, for many wannabe comics like Ellen, the crème de la crème of television appearances was on *The Tonight Show Starring*

Johnny Carson. Through the years, hilarious stand-ups such as Garry Shandling, Jerry Seinfeld, Roseanne Barr, Louie Anderson, Rita Rudner, Drew Carey, and others appeared on his legendary show and were launched to stand-up comedy superstardom. If Johnny Carson liked a particular comic's monologue, that comic was given a wave by Carson to join him over on the couch to chat for a few minutes. In an article about Carson's death in 2005, MTV writer Gil Kaufman explained how, "Those few minutes of banter were considered gold among comedians, both for their rarity and for the more important stamp of approval from Carson. Among the careers boosted by their appearances on *The Tonight Show* were Bill Cosby, Jerry Seinfeld, Richard Pryor and Rodney Dangerfield."[15]

Ed McMahon, Johnny Carson's longtime sidekick on *The Tonight Show,* once explained that he knew when Johnny was taking delight in a comedian's performance because, "he leaned on his left elbow with his wrist under his chin. When the comedian finished, that same hand waved him over to the couch and a career was sent into orbit. The comedian came to the couch to take my place and I moved down. That's how we knew when the show was over—when I reached the end of the couch."[16] However, up until the time that Ellen had arrived in Los Angeles, no female comedians had been waved over by Carson.

So Ellen hit the Los Angeles comedy circuit and performed at various clubs in the area. She kept her style of humor as it was—poking fun at life's situations. She also took her brand of humor to Sin City (Las Vegas) to perform at The Improv and once opened for comedian Franklyn Ajaye, aka "the Jazz Comedian," in 1986, who writes in his book *Comic Insights: The Art of Stand-up Comedy:*

> Ellen is a clever observational comedian with a distinctly light, offhand style of delivery. Her distinguishing characteristic—apart from the cleverness of her material—is her economical and clear setups. An effective setup is one of the most important tools that a comedian needs for his or her material to be successful because it gives the audience the context necessary for them to enjoy the punchline. Ellen has the ability to give an audience a clear picture of where she wants to take them with just a few

well-chosen words…I was struck then by her easy, con-
versational style of delivery, the sly self-effacing spin that
she put on her material, and the fact that gender didn't
seem to play much of a part in her choice of material.[17]

What Ellen brought to the Vegas Improv stage that night was
her "Phone Call to God" sketch. She nailed the routine, and it
paid off big time. Sitting in the audience was none other than Jim
McCawley, the then associate producer at *The Tonight Show Starring
Johnny Carson*, who told Ellen that Carson would love that bit. She
was subsequently booked for an appearance on the show. Ellen's
daydream was about to become a reality.

Ellen immediately called her mother, Betty, and screamed into
the phone about her appearance. She told her mother that the hard-
est part about this incredible opportunity was going to be performing in front of millions of viewers and not fainting dead away. Ellen
didn't faint dead away. Instead, she struck gold that night. Johnny
took delight in her performance and waved her over to sit on the
couch with him, the couch McMahon called "the cushioned rocket
to stardom."[18] Ellen was the first female comedian Carson ever invited for a chat on the couch of *The Tonight Show*. As expected, that
appearance catapulted her to superstardom and opened the coveted
Hollywood door for her.

NOTES

1. http://www.time.com/time/magazine/article/0,9171,986189,00.
html.

2. Transcript of *Primetime Live with Diane Sawyer*.

3. Betty DeGeneres, *Love, Ellen: A Mother/Daughter Journey* (New
York: William Morrow & Co., 1999), p. 122.

4. Transcript of *Primetime Live with Diane Sawyer*.

5. http://www.youtube.com/watch?v=76dpPbtJT84&feature=related.

6. http://www.tvweek.com/news/2008/01/from_hopeful_to_household_
name.php.

7. http://query.nytimes.com/gst/fullpage.html?res=9C0CE2D8103EF
930A25757C0A962958260&sec=&spon=&pagewanted=all.

8. http://www.people.com/people/ellen_degeneres/biography.

9. http://www.jeromefdn.org/templates/documents/press_releases/NYCJuly2007.pdf.

10. *The Advocate*, March 2000; http://findarticles.com/p/articles/mi_m1589/is_2000_March_14/ai_60021910/pg_6.

11. http://youtube.com/watch?v=fU4Yv7dI3uI.

12. *The San Francisco Chronicle*, November 30, 1986, Sunday datebook: p. 35.

13. http://query.nytimes.com/gst/fullpage.html?rcs=9C0CE2D8103EF930A25757C0A962958260&sec=&spon=&pagewanted=all.

14. http://query.nytimes.com/gst/fullpage.html?res=9C0CE2D8103EF930A25757C0A962958260&sec=&spon=&pagewanted=all.

15. http://www.mtv.com/news/articles/1496154/20050124/index.jhtml?headlines=true.

16. Ed McMahon, *Here's Johnny!: My Memories of Johnny Carson, The Tonight Show, and 46 Years of Friendship* (New York: Berkley, 2006), p. 136.

17. Franklyn Ajaye, *Comic Insights: The Art of Stand-up Comedy* (Los Angeles: Silman-James Press, 2002), p. 80.

18. Ed McMahon, *Here's Johnny!* p. 137.

Chapter 3

A FUNNY THING HAPPENED . . .

I ask people why they have deer heads on their walls. They always say
because it's such a beautiful animal. There you go. I think my mother
is attractive, but I have photographs of her.

—*Ellen DeGeneres*

Ellen performed on *The Tonight Show Starring Johnny Carson* an
impressive six times in just two years. Her natural comedic timing
earned her a minor role as the character Margo Van Meter on the Fox
television sitcom *Open House*, a 1989 spin-off of the Fox show *Duet*,
which ran for two seasons from 1987 to 1989 and focused on Ben,
the struggling mystery novelist; his girlfriend Laura, a caterer; and a
high-powered yuppie couple, Richard and Linda (played by Alison
LaPlaca). When the show ended, LaPlaca was given the lead in *Open
House*. According to *Variety*, *Open House* revolved around Linda
Phillips' work at the Juan Verde Real Estate office. At home, her husband cared for their daughter and pursued his career as a pianist.[1]

The Margo Van Meter character was written to be a man-hungry
secretary, and Ellen described the character as goofy, over the top,
and weird. Ellen used this role as an opportunity to learn the sitcom ropes, and she enjoyed the experience. When the show was
canceled after only one season, Ellen had nothing to worry about—
HBO had called.

In 1986, Ellen filmed her first HBO Special, *Young Comedians
Reunion*, with fellow comics Howie Mandel (in Toronto), Steven

Wright (Boston), Harry Anderson (Los Angeles), Richard Belzer (New York), and Robin Williams (San Francisco), each of whom performed from the cities where they first launched their career. Two years later, Ellen appeared in HBO's *Women of the Night*, an hour-long special with fellow female comedians Rita Rudner, Judy Tenuta, and Paula Poundstone.

Ellen's HBO special was well received by the critics. *Variety's* critic described Ellen as, "just keeps getting better and better. She is that rarity among stand-up comics: a true original. I'm not even sure if DeGeneres should be classified as a stand-up act; she's more comic actress. (And she's certainly the best thing on Fox TV's labored sitcom *Open House*.")[2] Critics, fans, and the television industry took notice of Ellen, and it only took a few more years for her to receive much-deserved accolades for her performances, including a CableACE nomination in 1989 for her appearance in the HBO Special *Command Performance: One Night Stand*. CableACE Awards honored achievements in cable programming that, at that time, were not eligible for the Emmy Awards. Ellen was also named "Best Female Stand-Up" at the 1991 American Comedy Awards.

In 1992, Ellen appeared on another short-lived television sitcom, ABC's *Laurie Hill*, as Nancy MacIntyre. *Laurie Hill* starred DeLane Matthews as Laurie, a typical working mother who tried to balance her roles as doctor, wife, and mother to a son, Leo. Unfortunately, the sitcom did not attract an audience and ran for only six episodes before it was pulled from the lineup.

In 1993, Ellen finally hit the big screen in a small way with a minor role in the feature film *Coneheads*, based on the *Saturday Night Live* sketch and starring Dan Aykroyd, Jane Curtin, and Laraine Newman (father, mother, and daughter, respectively). The Coneheads were an alien family, natives of the planet Remulak, who found themselves stranded on Earth. Although the sketch was a popular one on *SNL's* weekly schedule, it failed to translate as a major motion picture and failed to score big at the box office.

Although her stand-up was going well and Ellen garnered great reviews for her minor sitcom and film characters, she still couldn't land on a hit television show. It was even reported that Ellen turned down a role in the incredibly successful sitcom *Friends*, which ran for a decade and launched the careers of Matthew Perry, Courtney

Cox, David Schwimmer, Jennifer Aniston, and Matt LeBlanc into superstardom. Just when it seemed that all hope was lost of finding a successful sitcom that would highlight her comedy talents, there was a bright spot on the horizon.[3]

THESE FRIENDS OF MINE

The 1990s were the decade when television stations were eager to give rising comics their own half-hour sitcoms, and many became megahits. Bill Cosby's *The Cosby Show* ran an impressive eight years, from 1984 to 1992, and won multiple Emmy Awards, including best comedy. Roseanne Barr's *Roseanne* premiered in 1988 and won three Golden Globes, 40 additional awards, and 67 various nominations. Jerry Seinfeld's sitcom, *Seinfield,* premiered in 1990 on NBC and ran for nine years. It was honored with more than 20 major awards and nearly 60 nominations. Tim Allen's *Home Improvement* debuted in 1991 and won many Golden Globe Awards, 39 other awards, and 56 nominations. In 1995, ABC attempted another sitcom starring a comedian, the *Jeff Foxworthy Show,* but, unfortunately, the show was canceled after one season. It was renewed on another network, and canceled for good after that season. In 1996, *Everybody Loves Raymond,* based on the life of stand-up comic Ray Romano, premiered and stayed on the air for nine years, garnering numerous awards.

In 1994, Ellen was approached with the idea for her own sitcom from ABC Television and Disney. The industry wondered, however, how long they could keep up their success with a line of stand-up comic sitcoms. Would Ellen's show do as well? Or was the television audience tired of this type of show? ABC took the chance and signed Ellen to a half-hour sitcom originally called *These Friends of Mine* to be created by Neal Marlens and Carol Black, the writers behind the Emmy Award–winning hit *The Wonder Years.*

According to *The Complete Directory of Primetime Network and Cable TV Shows from 1946 to Present,* the original story line of *These Friends of Mine* was that "Ellen was a blonde, insecure somewhat hyper 30-something single who managed a Los Angeles bookstore/coffee shop called Buy the Book. Her original circle included Adam, her sloppy sarcastic roommate, a struggling photographer who was also playing the field; longtime friend Holly and smart-mouthed

Anita. They rated each other's dates, talked about their sexual misadventures (casual sex was big here) and how to dump people they didn't like."[4] One running gag for the show revolved around the theme song—each week there were different opening credits and music.

Ellen loved the pilot script. "I was laughing out loud when I read the script," she says. "I knew what I could do with it. I wanted to do a smarter, hipper version of *I Love Lucy*, only don't take it so far that I'm in a man's suit with a mustache trying to fool Ricky that I'm not his wife. I wanted a show that everybody talks about the next day."[5]

The first episode debuted on March 29, 1994, as a midsummer replacement, following fellow stand-up comic Tim Allen's sitcom *Home Improvement*, which was already enjoying a successful run. In the first episode of *These Friends of Mine*, Ellen renews her driver's license, but, in typical everyday fashion, the photos are horrible.

After its debut, critics talked and many compared *These Friends of Mine* to the already thriving *Seinfeld*, which although it was a show about the lives of several single friends, was also a self-described "show about nothing." *Entertainment Weekly* TV reviewer Ken Tucker wrote that *These Friends of Mine* was "an unnervingly self-conscious new sitcom," and that he hoped Ellen would "yet turn *These Friends of Mine* into something worthy of her. Watching her stand-up act, I've always thought of her as an exceptionally smart, unusually honest camp counselor, and what's most dispiriting about the pilot show is the way she has dimmed her usually bright-eyed, big-smiling countenance to approximate the patented Seinfeld deadpan."[6]

Atlanta Journal television critic Phil Kloer wrote, "*Friends* is, in fact, practically a parallel-universe version of *Seinfeld*, but with a female majority. Stand-up comic Ellen DeGeneres is the center, the one who wears a diamond necklace and formal black top to the DMV in a desperate attempt to get a decent driver's license photo. Although she has some of Seinfeld's obsessive-compulsiveness, she also has a goofy likeability that wears well."[7]

Ellen didn't think her show deserved the comparisons to *Seinfeld*. She didn't agree with the comparison that her show's plotline was about nothing. She saw her show as a cross between Mary Richards

(*Mary Tyler Moore*) and Lucy Ricardo (*I Love Lucy*). Ellen Morgan would get into physical situations like Lucy and want everything to work out okay, just like Mary Richards. But contrary to what the critics were writing about the comparisons to *Seinfeld*, Ellen's show was a ratings success. Ellen was even asked to start hosting award shows, including the Grammys. Ellen also cohosted the 46th *Annual Primetime Emmy Awards* in 1994 with Patricia Richardson, known mainly for her role as Jill Taylor on *Home Improvement*.

"Ellen's show had only been on the air for six episodes, and I took a lot of heat for that," said producer Don Mischer. "But [publicist] Pat Kingsley showed me a lot of things Ellen had done, and I met with her and had a gut feeling that she would do a great job. She scored. The night after the Emmys, no one was asking me why we hired her."[8]

Some of Ellen's funniest moments included talking to the bleacher people who couldn't see what was going on inside the venue. So Ellen recreated the events of the evening for the fans, including singing Bette Midler's songs from *Gypsy*. She also went into the press room—which included reporters who had phones up to their ears—and made it seem as if it were a telethon. "It was all classic DeGeneres shtick, and added just the right fizz to keep the show bubbling along at an amiable pace." Critics were pleased with Ellen's hosting duties, calling her the "roving reporter, going behind the scenes and into the audience for her occasionally laugh-out-loud observations."[9] For this performance, Ellen nabbed an American Comedy Award.

Sitting in the audience watching Ellen's first Emmy hosting performance were her father, Elliott, and her mom, Betty, who after divorcing Ellen's stepfather, was adjusting to life in her new Los Angeles digs. Betty kept herself busy working and doing volunteer work for various local organizations. She also appeared in promos for Ellen's sitcom and even had a bit role in one of Ellen's movies.

Meanwhile, Ellen's show was doing well in the ratings, but the station still felt that it needed some tweaking in order to maintain its longevity. Over the summer of 1994, ABC revamped the sitcom and focused less on the supporting characters and more on Ellen. The show was also moved to a new time slot following the highly successful *Roseanne*. There were conflicting tabloid reports as to whether Ellen, now becoming more successful and perhaps having more input on the show, initiated these changes. Reports claimed that either Ellen was unsatisfied with the quality of the first episodes or ABC made the decision to alter the story line and characters. The rumors turned out to be unfounded as the producers explained why they wanted to make these adjustments. "We all felt that Ellen was wonderful and that the show was working, but she could just use some more support comedically and personality-wise," said co-creator and executive producer David Rosenthal. "We're just trying to expand the show and broaden it. The major shift is that the show has really shifted from an ensemble to a show that really centers on a star and a character."[10]

In addition, a new team of writers and producers was hired to sharpen and focus the show. Writer-producer Mark Driscoll told *Television Week* how nobody on the show was certain the sitcom would survive after the first season, even though the ratings were good, since the sitcom lacked shape. With new producers Warren Bell and Suzanne Martin at the helm, the show seemed to gel. The studio enjoyed the new focus on Ellen's character. Ellen, in turn, was also happy with the changes, which made for a more relaxed atmosphere. As a result, the show garnered high ratings and praise.

Ellen Morgan would experience a minor metamorphosis in the new season. She was promoted to bookstore owner, and her close group of comrades was changed, as if the previous characters had packed up and moved away over the summer and new neighbors had moved in for the first episode of the new season. The character Holly was sent packing from the lineup because the producers felt the chemistry between Holly and Ellen Morgan just wasn't there. Actress Joely Fisher—the daughter of the legendary Connie Stevens—was introduced as Ellen's friend Paige Clark, and she soon became a heavy hitter in the show. Actor Arye Gross played Ellen's friend from college, Adam Green, and Clea Lewis portrayed Ellen's annoying friend Audrey Penney. The rest of the cast included Jeremy Piven, who was cast as Ellen's cousin Spence Kovak, and Alice Hirson and Steven Gilborn, who played Ellen's parents.

And there would be one more major change that season. The show returned in the fall of 1994 with a new name—it was simply *Ellen*. And based on the critics' reviews, it was simply a success as well—*TV Guide* later called *Ellen,* "a warm and funny slice-of-life sitcom."[11] "Of course, it helps to have a pleasing personality and a wholesome naturalness not often seen on sitcoms. Which brings us to Ellen DeGeneres, whose ABC comedy series *Ellen* has quickly become a bona fide hit, and stands as one of the few bright new spots on the fall schedule."[12]

Driscoll gave credit for the turnaround success to Ellen and her comedic timing. "She was always so funny when she came out and did her thing," he said. "She brought a lot to the performance. We loved her talent."[13]

Having a hit television show meant one thing for Ellen—her star potential shot through the roof, and she was offered a whopping one-million-dollar advance to write her first book, *My Point and I Do Have One,* published by Bantam Publishers. In her book she writes, "Dear Reader, I was awfully excited when I was asked to write a book. I was however, nervous. I was afraid I didn't have anything important to say. But when I began writing, I realized that although I don't know a lot about any one thing, I know a little about a whole bunch of things: baking a pie; dancing; curing the common cold; running the Iditarod—it's all in the book. And I realized I notice things that maybe some people don't notice (or they don't notice that they don't notice). That's all in the book too."[14]

Having a hit show did not mean that the book critics were going to be so kind about her writing. *Entertainment Weekly* book reviewer Lisa Schwarzbaum failed to see the point of Ellen's book and wrote, "I could hear DeGeneres saying (she was raised a Christian Scientist in New Orleans), 'A mil for 60,000 words? No sweat, I blab that much with my pals decompressing after each show.' It is because of such deeply misinformed thinking that DeGeneres hobbles through *My Point* like a novice Boston Marathoner. 'The lawyers have reminded me that the book must be at least 60,000 words,' she gasps, out of gas on the last chapter. She proceeds to limp to 'The End' announcing, 'Nothing has to mean anything; I can just look around and write down everything I'm looking at...' And she does."[15]

Another reviewer wrote, "Sadly, the pseudo-autobiography falls flat on its face even before the end of the first chapter. Perhaps DeGeneres' editor should have warned her that stand-up routines do not translate well to the printed page."[16]

Regardless of the critics lambasting the funny read, Ellen had the last laugh. Readers snatched up the manuscript; it premiered at the number one spot on the *New York Times* bestseller list, and it stayed on *Publishers Weekly*'s bestseller list for 24 weeks straight.

With Ellen's run of major success on television and now in print, she went for the trifecta again, and the film industry gave Ellen another shot at a hit feature film. She was cast in the lead of *Mr. Wrong*, a major motion picture about a lonely single woman, Martha Alston (played by Ellen), who finds the perfect man to date (played by Bill Pullman). However, when his Jekyll/Hyde personality erupts, she begins to regret her decision. Unfortunately, she can't convince anyone else how crazy he really is.

Mr. Wrong's director, Nick Castle, cast Ellen because he said she had an accessibility about her. He saw her as a pretty woman, but not a beauty queen, and observed that although Ellen was intelligent, she never talked down to anyone. Released in 1996, the film received mixed reviews—some critics called it "dreadful"; others said that Ellen had some funny moments, but the film wasn't enough to carry her talents. The *San Francisco Chronicle* reviewer said, "Despite a lively trailer and a pair of co-stars riding a wave of popularity, *Mr. Wrong* slipped into theaters largely unnoticed yesterday. It might as well slip right back out. *Mr. Wrong* is a dreadful movie—though you could be fooled for the first 30 minutes."[17] *Mr. Wrong* didn't last long in the theaters.

The movie wasn't a blockbuster, and unlike other comedians who made a triumphant switch from television to film—such as Jim Carrey (from *In Living Color* to *Ace Ventura: Pet Detective*) or Tim Allen (from *Home Improvement* to *The Santa Clause*)—Ellen lost the attempt at a successful triple play. She still had a number one bestselling book and her thriving sitcom that started to include special guest appearances, including *Jeopardy*'s Alex Trebek, Martha Stewart, Ron Palillo (Horshack on *Welcome Back Kotter*), Carrie Fisher, country music star Trisha Yearwood, and more. The comedian was happy about where she was in her career and joked, "Every day I pinch myself because I'm sure I must be dreaming. Actually I don't pinch myself. It's one of my manager's jobs to pinch me and say, 'You ain't dreamin' kid!' Then I pinch, he pinches me back and it usually ends up in a slap fight. Sometimes the slap fight lasts until midnight. Then we call it a day, go to sleep and repeat it all again the next morning."[18]

The *Ellen* show would undergo more character and plot changes in the third season, while the producers continued to keep the show on pace with its success. Over the course of the season, the Buy the Book bookstore was destroyed in an earthquake, but instead of rebuilding, Ellen Morgan sold the store to a franchise but stayed on as its manager. Ellen's new roommate was her cousin Spence, and Audrey, the giggly airheaded friend, was introduced. Season three was a ratings success.

And Ellen experienced something new with the success of her show—the tabloids' overzealous interest in the offscreen Ellen and her personal life. The paparazzi wanted to know more about this private comedian, especially who she was dating at any given time. Since Ellen had not officially come out yet, this invasiveness ended up being a difficult adjustment period for her. Photographers were taking pictures and writing unflattering captions. Writers were misquoting her. "The first time it happened, I was freaked out, and I wondered how can I get on television and tell everybody that this isn't true. Now, I realize it's not personal. They have a job to do and that's how they sell papers. That's what they do, they make up stories, and I'm flattered that I'm a big enough name that they're making up stories on me...At one time, they wouldn't have written anything about me, and now they're finding all kinds of stuff to write about me."[19]

Ellen also confessed that losing her privacy as she gained celebrity was a scary thought and joked that when she had enough celebrity and loss of privacy, she'd move to Montana. Not only would Ellen continue to walk the fine line of letting her fans know more about her and maintaining a private life, but her private life was about to become one of the most watched story lines both on and off the television screen.

NOTES

1. http://www.variety.com/profiles/TVSeries/Synopsis/158628/Open+House.html?dataSet=1.

2. *The Times-Picayune*, February 18, 1990; Section: TV FOCUS; p. T50.

3. http://www.people.com/people/ellen_degeneres.

4. Tim Brooks, *The Complete Directory of Primetime Network and Cable TV Shows from 1946 to Present* (New York: Ballantine Books, 2003), p. 416.

5. http://query.nytimes.com/gst/fullpage.html?res=9C0CE2D8103EF930A25757C0A962958260&sec=&spon=&pagewanted=2.

6. http://www.ew.com/ew/article/0,,301584,00.html.

7. Phil Kloer, "These Friends of Mine," *The Atlanta Constitution*, Features, p. D1.

8. http://www.highbeam.com/doc/1G1-174206163.html.

9. *Daily Breeze* (Torrance, CA), p. C3, September 12, 1994.

10. *Corpus Christi Caller-Times*, Texas, p. B7, December 13, 1994.

11. http://www.tvguide.com/tvshows/ellen/100136.

12. *The Oregonian* (Portland, OR), sec. Television, p. D09, September 1, 1994.

13. Ibid.

14. Ellen DeGeneres, *My Point and I Do Have One* (New York: Bantam, 1995), back cover.

15. http://www.ew.com/ew/article/0,,298566,00.html.

16. http://www.curledup.com/mypoint.htm.

17. http://www.sfgate.com/cgi-bin/article.cgi?f=/c/a/1996/02/17/DD3386.DTL.

18. Ellen DeGeneres, *My Point and I Do Have One*, p. 57.

19. Kathleen Tracy, *Ellen: The Real Story of Ellen DeGeneres* (New York: Pinnacle, 2005), p. 167.

Chapter 4

THE PUPPY EPISODE

I gotta work out. I keep saying it all the time. I keep saying I gotta start working out. It's been about two months since I've worked out. And I just don't have the time. Which uh...is odd. Because I have the time to go out to dinner. And uh...and watch TV. And get a bone density test. And uh...try to figure out what my phone number spells in words.

—Ellen DeGeneres

In 1996, the fourth season of the hit sitcom *Ellen* didn't get off on the right track—the ratings of the show's season opener dropped 27 percent from the previous year, and critics were already harping that the show was getting stale. Producers even hinted that another shake-up was on the horizon.[1] Behind the scenes, Ellen DeGeneres had thought long and hard about having her character, Ellen Morgan, finally come out of the closet and admit her preferred sexuality. She even talked to her mom, who was concerned that Ellen might be jeopardizing her entire career. Some gossip publications suggested that the producers had thrown the idea around for years. *Entertainment Weekly* also reported that former staffers said Ellen DeGeneres wasn't ready to come out yet and was nervous about anything that hinted of her character's lesbianism, including one episode in which Ellen schemes about how to become better friends with a woman she has just met. Tabloids reported that Ellen was uncomfortable with some suggestive scenes and had them rewritten.[2]

Thanks to media pressure and the fact that Ellen wanted to be true to herself, she began exploring the idea of coming out with her television persona and in real life. "The only reason I did that is because, you know, the press—no offense—is very inquisitive, and I was constantly trying to dodge questions and hide. And I just didn't want to do that anymore. I didn't want to feel a sense of shame," she said. "So I decided to come out really for personal reasons, then the show kind of, you know, it seemed like a fun idea to do with the show. I was very naive in thinking it wouldn't be a big deal. It was a huge deal."[3]

Perhaps it was easier to make this proclamation through Ellen's on-screen character first, or perhaps by announcing that Ellen Morgan was gay, Ellen DeGeneres could relate more to Ellen Morgan, something that the producers believed might be missing from the show. Maybe once Ellen's character came out of the closet, the show's ratings would gain a boost. Ted Harbert, a production executive with DreamWorks and former president of ABC Entertainment who developed *Ellen* for the network, said that asking Ellen to portray a straight woman was the wrong thing to do. It was becoming more noticeable that the character Ellen Morgan didn't have chemistry with her male dates on the show, and marrying her off wasn't a possibility. "The same thing that applies to *Ellen* applies to every other situation comedy: who you are as a person comes through that glass screen," said Harbert. "All the big sitcom stars, from Lucille Ball to Jerry Seinfeld, basically played who they are. We asked Ellen to do a very hard thing, which was play something other than who she was. It created problems from the start."[4]

When Ellen finally announced her decision to her staff to make the pivotal character change during this season, the producers' positive feedback was exciting. Mark Driscoll, who had been writing for the show since it premiered as *These Friends of Mine* in 1994 and was promoted to executive producer, was thrilled and knew that this was the missing piece to a hit show.

However, convincing ABC and Disney—a family-oriented company—was going to be a difficult task. Ellen met with Dean Valentine, president of Disney Television, and Jamie Tarses, the head of ABC Entertainment (who had orchestrated the lesbian wedding on NBC's sitcom *Friends*). While the meetings were top secret, it was joked that Ellen should get a puppy. "Yeah. That's good," recalls executive producer Mark Driscoll. "It was an indication of just how lost the show was that they would be excited by Ellen buying a puppy."[5] Once the episode was approved, and as an inside joke, the writers titled the Ellen-comes-out show as "The Puppy Episode."[6] Ellen teased the media about the coming out and dropped not-so-subtle hints of what was about to happen. According to GLAAD, Ellen appeared as a guest on *The Rosie O'Donnell Show* and said jokingly that her alter-ego, Ellen Morgan, would be coming out on her sitcom later in the season: "Yes, the rumors are true; we'll be revealing that my character is Llll...ebanese, because she enjoys both baba ganoush and Casey Kasem." GLAAD also reported that O'Donnell, who had not yet come out publicly, responded by saying that since she is also a big fan of Casey Kasem, "maybe I'm Lebanese, too." Ellen told Rosie that she thought she might be Lebanese.[7] Ellen would also answer reporters' questions with, "No, we're adding a new character named Les Bian."[8]

Jennifer Reed, contributor to *Queer Popular Culture: Literature, Media, Film and Television*, was excited about the prospect that both Ellens were coming out: "This was very exciting news for this lesbian, and for many of my queer friends. The hints and rumors worked very well to get us to watch for what would come next. The excitement was inseparable from our unconfirmed knowledge, our assumption that Ellen DeGeneres was herself a lesbian. Taken together, this created a very queer atmosphere. It was based mostly on the open secret, the wink, the anticipation—and it played itself out both on the show and in the media about the show."[9]

In 1997, Ellen told talk show host Larry King that the media and viewer tease was not supposed to last almost the entire season. Instead, it was supposed to be short term, with the coming out episode as episode 10. Instead, waiting for approval from the corporation pushed the launch date back further and further, so the teasing continued.

However, once television critics got word that there would be a gay main character on the show, they expressed concern as to whether the show would succeed. Rich Heldenfels of Knight Ridder Newspapers explained that making Ellen Morgan gay wouldn't necessarily make her—or the show—funny: "Having a gay character doesn't make *Spin City* a good show or *Mad About You* a bad one. The same thing applies to *Ellen*. Everyone involved needs to figure out how a gay Ellen Morgan makes this show better, even if the publicity brings people to the show, they won't come back if what they see isn't funny."[10]

Ellen and the producers decided that Ellen Morgan's coming out would take place during a special one-hour season finale on April 30, 1997. "For me," she said, "this has been the most freeing experience because people can't hurt me anymore. I don't have to worry about somebody saying something about me, or a reporter trying to find out information...I don't have anything to be scared of, which I think outweighs whatever else happens in my career."[11]

Fellow comedians thought that Ellen was making the right move, too. "She's one of the funniest women on the planet," says lesbian comic Suzanne Westenhoefer. "But the show's been mediocre at best. [Ellen's coming out] would be Christmas for gay people."[12] Unfortunately, not everyone felt as free about the decision as Ellen did, and she started to get a sample of what the backlash to her life-altering decision might be. The *San Jose Mercury News* quoted L. Brent Bozzell III, founder of Alexandria, Virginia–based Media Research Center, who said Ellen Morgan's coming out created a sense of horror. Bozzell rallied big names in the Christian conservative movement against the coming out of Ellen Morgan. He believed a majority of viewers were appalled that "there are some elements in Hollywood who are bent, come hell or high water, on thrusting garbage down the throats of children. The world is full of decent homosexuals," Bozell said. "That's not the issue. The issue is their lifestyle. By portraying that lifestyle as perfectly normal, decent and acceptable, an indecency is being perpetuated."[13]

It was hard to understand the negative reaction to a gay television character when, after all, Ellen DeGeneres wasn't the first to portray a gay character on television. In 1977, comedian Billy Crystal played Jodie Dallas, a gay man, on the ABC sitcom *Soap*, a weekly half-hour prime-time comedy. There was a tremendous amount of backlash, which involved the mobilization of several organizations that were against the show, including the Christian Life Commission of the Southern Baptist Convention, the International Union of Gay Athletes, and the National Gay Task Force.

Also mobilized were the National Council of Churches, the United Church of Christ, the United Methodist Church, and the National Council of Catholic Bishops, although they asked the members of their 138,000 collective churches to watch the show first and then inform ABC of their feelings about it. Nonetheless, reports showed that the network received 32,000 letters of complaint before the show's premiere, and 8 out of 195 ABC affiliates refused to air the show.[14]

Other popular sitcoms also featured gay characters—although not necessarily in lead roles—including *All in the Family* (female impersonator Beverly La Salle); *The Golden Girls*; *Mary Hartman, Mary Hartman*; *Dynasty*; *The Tracey Ullman Show*; and more. In 1991, the award-winning longtime drama *L.A. Law* featured a kiss between two women characters, portrayed by actresses Michelle Greene and Amanda Donohoe. According to the *New York Times*, when the CBS series *Picket Fences* showed a kiss between two teenage girls, the network insisted the scene be shot in semidarkness.[15]

One sitcom that created quite a stir over a gay-themed episode was *Roseanne*, an Emmy Award–winning sitcom on ABC from 1988 to 1997 starring stand-up comic Roseanne Barr, who portrayed Roseanne Conner. In a 1994 episode, Roseanne Conner visited a gay bar for the first time with her bisexual friend Nancy (who was played by comedian Sandra Bernhard). During the episode, Roseanne innocently danced with a woman, played by Mariel Hemingway, and when they took a break and sat at a table, Hemingway kissed her.

ABC threatened not to air the episode, but Roseanne stood her ground and insisted that she would take the episode to another network. ABC withdrew their threat and aired the episode with a viewer advisory. The ratings for the show were high—approximately 33 million viewers—and the complaints were lower than originally anticipated.[16]

On the long-running sitcom *Friends*, Ross's ex-wife left him for another woman. On January 18, 1996, *Friends* ran the episode "The One with the Lesbian Wedding," in which Ross's lesbian ex-wife, Carol, married her lover, Susan, in a wedding officiated by Candice Gingrich, the gay sister of the then House Speaker Newt Gingrich. In his book, *Gay TV and Straight America*, author Ron Becker explains how running this episode during that television season was anticlimactic since there were many other gay-themed television shows.

Regardless of the prevalence of gay characters in recent television sitcoms and dramas, Ellen Morgan's coming out was a landmark moment in television history. *Ellen* would be the first television show to feature a gay lead actress in a sitcom. It didn't come without its opponents, though. Similar to what happened with *Soap,* antigay activists launched their own campaign to keep the *Ellen* episode off the air. Organizations associated with the religious right took out a full page ad in *Variety* condemning the show. Advertisers— including Chrysler and J.C. Penney—cancelled their sponsorship of the show. Reverend Donald E. Wildmon and his American Family Association issued threats to boycott advertisers of the show as well. Televangelist Jerry Falwell resorted to name calling and labeled the comedian "Ellen DeGenerate," to which Ellen responded, "Really, he called me that? Ellen DeGenerate? I've been getting that since fourth grade. I guess I'm happy I could give him work."[17]

By the time the show ran, one affiliate, ABC 33/40 in Birmingham, Alabama, refused to show the historic episode. After the taping of the final episode, someone called in a bomb threat, and the studios were evacuated.[18]

To combat the negativity, GLAAD worked with a local Birmingham gay pride organization to help 3,000 local fans watch the banned telecast via satellite. They launched a "Let Ellen Out!" campaign to create grassroots support and developed Ellen Watch, a Web page dedicated to following the title character's journey in her coming out process. GLAAD organized "Come Out with Ellen" house parties in more than 1,500 households nationwide and signature parties in New York; Los Angeles; Washington, D.C.; Kansas City, Missouri; and San Francisco. These parties brought together more than 4,000 people and the *Ellen* cast to watch the event live.

Ellen's brother, Vance, was more concerned about her safety. However, he hoped that Ellen would achieve her goals with this episode and send a positive message about the gay and lesbian community to the American public.

Cast to play Ellen's love interest, Susan, was famed actress Laura Dern, the daughter of actor Bruce Dern and actress Diane Ladd. Laura had been involved in acting since she was young and had roles in such movies as *Mask, Smooth Talk, Blue Velvet,* and *Wild at Heart.* She earned an Oscar nod for her role in *Rambling Rose.* She also played Ellie Sattler in two of the *Jurassic Park* movies. Dern wasn't the only celebrity to make an appearance in this momentous episode. The episode actually became a who's who of Hollywood, with guest stars such as Demi Moore, Melissa Etheridge, k.d. lang, Dwight Yoakum, Billy Bob Thornton, and Oprah Winfrey (who played Ellen's therapist).

"It was 7 P.M. (three days before filming), and someone says there is someone on the phone claiming to be Oprah Winfrey. I pick up the phone expecting it to be a hoax, and I hear Tammy? Oprah! and we begin to discuss the possibility. This is one of the 25 most influential people in America, so once we got her we knew the potential was gonna be huge," said Tamara Billick, casting director.[19]

"Huge" was the understatement of the year, but not everyone thought that the episode would be a good thing. *Time* magazine asked various creators and producers for their opinions. Dick Wolf, creator of *Law & Order,* predicted that *Ellen* would suffer from the change. Bruce Helford, producer of Drew Carey's sitcom, admitted that he wouldn't have been so bold, calling it only a temporary spike in the ratings if the rest of the show still isn't funny.[20] Only time would tell.

NOTES

1. EW.com/ew/article/0,,294355?5,00.html?print.

2. http://www.ew.com/ew/article/0,,294355_4,00.html?print.

3. *The Post-Standard* (Syracuse, NY), April 20, 2003, Stars section p. 4.

4. Verne Gay, "All About Ellen," *Newsday* (Melville, NY), Nassau and Suffolk, Part II, B08, April 24, 1997.

5. http://www.newsweek.com/id/109133/output/print.

6. Ibid.

7. http://www.usatoday.com/life/2002/2002-03-12-rosie.htm.

8. http://www.ew.com/ew/article/0,,294355,00.html.

9. Jennifer Reed, contributor, *Queer Popular Culture: Literature, Media, Film and Television* (Houndmills: Palgrave Macmillan, 2007), p. 12.

10. *Kansas City Star,* FYI, p. F6, October 16, 1996.

11. www.time.com/time/printout—Monday, April 14, 1997.

12. http://www.ew.com/ew/article/0,,294355_4,00.html?print.

13. *San Jose Mercury News* (CA), Morning Final, sec. Silicon Valley Life, p. 1E, April 30, 1997.

14. http://query.nytimes.com/gst/fullpage.html?res=950DE3DE103DF937A15757C0A96F948260.

15. http://query.nytimes.com/gst/fullpage.html?res=940CEEDD1438F93AA35751C0A962958260.

16. Nightlines, Windy City Times, *Chicago Sun-Times* Feb.-March, 1994.

17. Rick Marin and Sue Miller, "Ellen Steps Out; Here Comes TV's First Leading Lesbian," *Newsweek*, April 14, 1997, p. 64–67.

18. Ibid.

19. http://ellen.4thdimension.info/modules.php?name=Sections&op=viewarticle&artid=136.

20. http://www.time.com/time/printout/0,8816,986188,00.html#.

Chapter 5

"YEP, I'M GAY"

I never wanted to be the lesbian actress. I never wanted to be the
spokesperson for the gay community. Ever. I did it for my own truth.

—*Ellen DeGeneres*, Time *magazine article, 1997*

NICE TO MEET YOU, MR. PRESIDENT

Fictional Ellen Morgan was about to come out of the closet to a tall,
long-haired blond character named Susan and to millions of people
watching and scrutinizing her every move. At the same time, Ellen
DeGeneres was also about to come out to millions of people who
were watching and scrutinizing her every move, while gracing the
cover of the April 14, 1997, *Time* magazine with the words, "Yep,
I'm Gay."

It was in this article that Ellen openly talked about her life as a
gay woman and a closeted gay comedian. Writer Bruce Handy asked
Ellen about the difficulties of being a closeted comedian. "You can
imagine the fag jokes," Ellen responded. "I would always follow
somebody doing either dyke jokes or fag jokes and doing the lisp
thing and the audience is going crazy and laughing. I just thought,
'Oh God. What if they pick up that I'm gay?'"[1]

They didn't, and Ellen kept her secret for many years. After
she revealed that she was gay, everybody was watching what Ellen
would do next. After "The Puppy Episode" aired on April 30, 1997,

Ellen made her first public appearance as a gay woman with a short-haired blonde actress named Anne Heche on her arm—at the White House.

Anne Heche was born May 25, 1969, in Aurora, Ohio. She grew up wanting to be an actress and was offered a contract to appear on the long-running soap opera *As the World Turns* when she was 16 years old, but she and her mother felt it best that she finish high school first. After graduation, Anne went on to pursue her career playing the Emmy Award–winning dual roles of Vicky Hudson and Marley Love Hudson on *Another World* from 1987 to 1991. Anne moved to the big screen with roles in many movies, including *Donnie Brasco*, *Wag the Dog*, *Six Days Seven Nights*, and the remake of the legendary thriller *Psycho*. Socially, Anne was known as a heterosexual woman who dated comedian Steve Martin for a few years.

Ellen and Anne had met briefly and were reacquainted at a party when Anne found her to be "the most ravishing woman I had seen. She was standing there in a gorgeous ice blue suit and radiating such confidence and beauty, I knew I had to spend more time with her."[2] Anne told her friend at that party that Ellen would be someone she would be in a relationship with someday.

In her autobiography, *Call Me Crazy*, published in 2001, Anne tells how Ellen didn't want to date a straight woman who was experimenting with being gay, but Anne assured her that her feelings were real. It was a particularly sensitive time in Ellen's career. The rumors about Ellen Morgan were spreading like wildfire, and watercooler talk was brewing. From this point on, what real-life Ellen DeGeneres did in public would be watched carefully, and Ellen wanted Anne to realize what she was getting into.

Anne welcomed the relationship, even seeing it as something brought on by fate. In her book, Anne relates that on their first date, when Anne saw Ellen's home, she thought it was a sign from above that their relationship should move forward. Anne explained to Ellen that the house Ellen lived in was once the house that Steve Martin almost bought for her. Ellen told Anne that she had heard the story about Steve and an ex-girlfriend but didn't realize the ex-girlfriend was Anne.[3]

Ellen's mother, Betty, liked Anne, too, and thought that the pair were happy together—something that Ellen needed at that time.

Betty once said of Anne, "I claim her. I say I have two daughters. Anne calls me Momma. I call them 'the twins.' They look exactly alike. I took a picture of them from the back, and you can't tell them apart. I met all of Ellen's girlfriends, and this is absolutely it. As Anne says, their souls were meant to be together."[4]

THE EPISODE

Ellen had the support of her family and friends and her girlfriend Anne. Betty even had a walk-on role in the pivotal episode of *Ellen* as a passenger at the airport. In "The Puppy Episode," Ellen is visited by her old boyfriend, Richard, and his female boss, Susan. Ellen becomes attracted to Susan. She has dinner with Richard but is unable to have an intimate encounter with him later. Instead, she winds up in a late-night conversation with Susan, who suggests she might be gay. Ellen discusses these developments with her therapist (played by Oprah Winfrey) and makes the decision to come out to her friends. Not all her friends take the revelation well. Ellen's friend Paige struggles with the idea that her friend is gay, and Ellen struggles with her own feelings and the reactions of her family and friends. During the episode, Ellen has an amusing dream in which she is grocery shopping and various employees and shoppers are offering her "lesbian specials."

Once Ellen decides to tell Susan that she has feelings for her, she finds out that Susan and Richard are leaving town that night. Thinking she won't have another chance, Ellen rushes to the airport to tell Susan how she feels. She admits to Susan that she has been thinking about what she said the night before and that Susan was right. At first, Ellen can't bring herself to say the words *I'm gay*, and she tearfully wonders why it's so difficult. "I think emotionally the most difficult scene to rehearse was when Ellen said she was gay, because literally every time we'd do that scene she would burst into tears," said Gill Junger, director.[5]

A few moments later, Ellen Morgan finds the strength to just blurt out the words, and as she turns to do so, she does not realize that she is standing directly in front of the airport microphone. The words *I'm gay* are echoed throughout the entire terminal. The studio audience erupts in applause. The extras in the airport scene look shocked (look for Betty DeGeneres in this scene). Ellen, feeling relieved about what she has just done, says goodbye to Susan only to discover that it is Richard, not Susan, who is really leaving. Susan has a three-day stay in the area, and the two head off to have coffee. The scene ends with a shot of Ellen Morgan smiling.

The off-camera smiles continued over the next few months as well. Writer Josh Ozersky called it "one of the publicized pseudo-events in TV history," but it worked.[6] The ratings numbers broke records—"The Puppy Episode" was seen by 42 million people, making it the most-watched program of that week and ABC's most-watched program of the season. Both ABC and Disney were pleased with the numbers. "We're very proud. We think Ellen and the show's staff have executed it beautifully," says Jamie Tarses, president of ABC Entertainment. At the same time, she adds, "obviously this is an experiment. We're not sociologists. We don't know how this is going to be received."[7]

Ellen would earn multiple awards for "The Puppy Episode," including an Emmy for Outstanding Writing and a Peabody Award. The series was also awarded a GLAAD Media Award for Outstanding TV Comedy Series. Ellen was also named "Entertainer of the Year" for 1997 by *Entertainment Weekly. EW* writes, "At a time when an acknowledgment of homosexuality has entered all aspects of popular culture, when diversity and acceptance are the words of the day but by no means entirely the deeds, and when more and more of the sizable population of homosexual men and women working in the entertainment industry today are weighing the risks of coming out themselves, DeGeneres allowed herself to become a poster girl—not for lesbianism, but for honesty."[8] The following year, on April 19, 1998, Ellen was honored at the 9th Annual GLAAD Media Awards with the Stephen F. Kolzak Award, presented to an openly LGBT media professional who has made a significant difference in promoting equal rights for the community.

In the months following the episode, America had time to digest what had happened. While televangelists and others antigay protesters knocked Ellen down, there were those who sang her praises for her bold move. *Newsweek* writer Jonathan Alter, in an article about then vice president Al Gore, wrote, "Ann Lewis, White

House communications director, says that *Ellen* is simply a mirror of reality—millions of Americans are gay or have family and friends who are (including Lewis, whose brother, Barney Frank, is an openly gay member of Congress). Of those who object to *Ellen*, Lewis says: 'They've got a problem with reality.'"[9]

While talking to the Hollywood Radio and Television Society, Gore championed *Ellen*, saying "when the character Ellen came out, millions of Americans were forced to look at sexual orientation in a more open light." These comments triggered another derogatory response from Falwell, "[Vice President Gore] recently praised the lesbian actress who plays 'Ellen' on ABC Television...I believe he may even put children, young people, and adults in danger by his public endorsement of deviant homosexual behavior...Our elected leaders are attempting to glorify and legitimize perversion."[10]

LEND A HELPING HAND

While Ellen was fighting for her right to be who she was both on television and off, Betty DeGeneres was getting involved in causes on behalf of her daughter. After meeting Tammy Billik, the casting director on *Ellen*, Betty was introduced to the executive director of the Human Rights Campaign (HRC) and began to volunteer. She eventually became the first nongay national spokesperson for the HRC's Coming Out Project, an ongoing campaign to encourage and assist gay people in being honest about their lives, provide guidance to campus groups and individuals dealing with coming out, and sponsor National Coming Out Day events. As the HRC's National Coming Out spokesperson, Betty appeared in television public service announcements and spoke throughout the country to promote honesty about being gay or, as in her case, having a gay family member and supporting equal rights for gay people.

"The fact that Betty is a concerned mom underscores the point that ending discrimination based on sexual orientation is not just of interest to gay people," says HRC Executive Director Elizabeth Birch. "It's a family issue that all Americans have a stake in."[11] Betty would also become an active member of Parents, Family and Friends of Lesbians and Gays (PFLAG).

OUT, BUT FUNNY?

The expectations of Ellen both on- and off-screen during the months after the revelation were high. "That's potent, provocative TV and the range of pop culture has been permanently expanded by it...*Ellen* also made (the *Boston Globe*'s) list of 1997's top TV for artistic reasons. When Ellen Morgan came out, the series grew overnight from an amiable sitcom into a show that's as witty as it is mind-expanding."[12]

Not all critics were as favorable about the show's new plotlines. Caryn James of the *New York Times* Critic's Notebook said that Ellen wasn't much funnier out of the closet than in: "The final episode, called 'Ellen: A Hollywood Tribute,' demonstrates all the worst aspects of the show this year: It is annoyingly self-important and preachy."[13]

THEY'RE WATCHING YOU

All Ellen wanted to do was to make people laugh and, through her character, illustrate the life of a gay woman who has just come out of the closet. However, just because she opened that door did not mean that her battles were over and everything would be smooth sailing from there. For most of the fifth season, ABC labeled the sitcom with a rating of TV-14. However, one episode triggered a harsher rating by ABC. In that episode there would be a joking kiss between Ellen and Paige. As a result, ABC added a cautionary warning label to the show that stated, "Due to adult content, parental discretion is advised." Ellen was not pleased with this rating, especially with all of the straight sex scenes on television, and threatened to quit the show.[14]

In her private life, Anne understood that Ellen was being scrutinized by conservatives and the media. Anne was soon to get her own bird's-eye view of discrimination, when her new movie, *Volcano*, was released. Anne wanted to attend the premiere with Ellen as her girlfriend. Unfortunately, Anne's "people" such as her managers and agent did not want Anne to do this and asked her to keep the relationship under wraps for just a few more weeks until papers were signed on her next movie. They believed that the thriving actress was in danger of sacrificing her career by being in a homosexual relationship. Anne was completely taken aback. "I never realized the media frenzy was going to be as big as it was," said Anne. "People who supposedly knew me were saying, 'could you just be a little less of who you are for a couple of days, could you just not show up at the premier of your movie with your new girl-friend or whatever you want to call it and just sign the deal for your next movie before you are really open about it.'"[15] Anne signed her next deal, to costar with Harrison Ford as the leading lady in *Six Days Seven Nights*.

Anne would soon be outed, however, when she and Ellen made headlines while attending the White House Correspondents' Dinner. The White House Correspondents' Association (WHCA) is an organization of journalists who cover stories on the president of the United States, and the dinner has been an annual tradition since 1920. When the couple were introduced to then president Bill Clinton, they posed for pictures with him. Like anyone in a relationship might do, Ellen placed her arm around Anne. The next day, the pictures were distributed through the media outlets. The *New York Times* described her behavior as an "ostentatious display of affection with her lover in front of President Clinton."[16]

Bruce Vilanch, a columnist for *The Advocate*, responded to the *New York Times*' comments in the June 24, 1997, edition: "And in real life if Ellen wants to fall in love with a flamboyant individual she has nothing to be ashamed of, nothing to hide. If she wants to show her off and be proud of her and introduce her to the president of the United States, she has no reason not to. I'll bet those beltway newlyweds Andrea Mitchell and Alan Greenspan were photographed holding hands that night at the same White House dinner. Would they be slimed for it? We mustn't set a series of double standards for ourselves."[17]

Dana Kennedy, who wrote an article analyzing Ellen and Anne's relationship and the effect it would have on their Hollywood careers, interviewed the producer of *Six Days, Seven Nights* about Anne's lesbian relationship. He was concerned that it would change the audience's perception of the movie, even going so far as to say that it might have become a joke that Anne was romancing Harrison Ford. In the same article, Kennedy quotes another female studio executive who said, "Knowing too much ruins the fantasy. She'll never be able to play a dramatic leading-lady role. [She can play] no believable love scenes with a man anymore." Would others disagree? Maybe, but Anne's career would go through more bizarre twists and turns over the next few years.

NOTES

1. http://www.time.com/time/magazine/article/0,9171,986189,00. html.

2. Anne Heche, *Call Me Crazy* (New York: Washington Square Press, 2003), p. 211.

3. Ibid.

4. Gail Shister, "Up with People," *Pittsburgh Post-Gazette* (PA), sec. Arts & Entertainment, p. 40, March 13, 1998.

5. http://ellen.4thdimension.info/modules.php?name=Sections&op= viewarticle&artid=136.

6. Susan J. Hubert, "What's Wrong with this Picture? The Politics of Ellen's Coming Out Party," *Journal of Popular Culture* 33/2 (1999): 31–36.

7. http://www.time.com/time/magazine/article/0,9171,986188–3,00. html.

8. http://www.ew.com/ew/article/0,,290814,00.html.

9. www.newsweek.com/id/97239/output/print.

10. http://www.hatecrime.org/subpages/hatespeech/robertson.html.

11. http://findarticles.com/p/articles/mi_qa3693/is_199710/ai_ n8767489.

12. *Boston Globe*, p. D6, December 28, 1997.

13. http://query.nytimes.com/gst/fullpage.html?res=9E01E2D61F31F93 1A25756C0A96E958260&sec=&spon=&pagewanted=2.

14. http://query.nytimes.com/gst/fullpage.html?res=9E04E7DB173CF9 3AA35753C1A961958260.

15. Anne Heche, *Call Me Crazy*, p. 213.

16. *New York Times*, Acceptable Affection, May 1.

17. Bruce Vilanch, "The Happy Couple—Lesbian Pair Ellen DeGeneres and Anne Heche," *The Advocate*, June 24, 1997.

Chapter 6

THE AFTERMATH

The following season, ratings for *Ellen* were dropping fast. A show that once had a modestly successful following, with almost 40 million viewers who witnessed the coming out of its main character, was averaging only 12 million viewers a week, which in Hollywood terms was a dangerous fall. But why? What was the reason that audiences didn't want to watch *Ellen* anymore? Was it because Ellen Morgan was gay? Was it the writing? Was *Ellen* still funny?

The answer depended on who you asked. Chastity Bono, the daughter of legendary singers Cher and Sonny Bono, and a lesbian who had come out, was also the entertainment director at the time for GLAAD. In remarks published in the *San Jose Mercury News*, Chastity was quoted as saying the *Ellen* show went from having no gay jokes to being "too gay-specific" to attract a large audience. "A lot of the stuff on it is somewhat of an inside joke," Bono was quoted as saying. "It's one thing to have a gay lead character, but it's another when every episode deals with pretty specific gay issues."[1]

Ellen was hurt by comments about the show being too gay: "But I don't know. I was always shocked by [people saying *Ellen* was too gay]. I don't think my show was too gay. It was gay. That's what it was. They just wanted to put 'too' in front of gay to make it sound like it was an extreme. It was weird because back then a lot of gay people were saying, 'You're not gay enough.' What am I then? Straight people think I'm too gay. Gay people don't think

I'm gay enough. I'm just gay. I just said that I was gay. And now suddenly I have to be the perfect gay person."[2]

In *The Advocate*, Bono explained that it looked like she called up *Variety* and began attacking Ellen, "which I would never do," she said. "I was merely theorizing as to the different reasons why the ratings are down, and the reporter honed in on that and twisted it. It's not indicative of how I feel at all." The article also claimed that Joan Garry, executive director of GLAAD, said the article "clearly misrepresents Chastity's good work."[3] Chastity insisted that the quotes were taken out of context, but the damage was already done.

Despite the lower ratings, Ken Tucker of *Entertainment Weekly* loved the beginning of the new season: "It's often said that you can't be funny if you're also trying to promote a social or political agenda; the urge to proselytize is supposed to lead inexorably to sourpuss humorlessness. But *Ellen*, now in its fifth season, keeps getting funnier, even as its star conducts the most relentless gay-empowerment campaign prime time has ever seen. So far the triumph of the show's new season is that while the majority of its punchlines are about homosexuality, the subject hasn't become predictable or dull—pretty amazing, given how many jokes it takes to fill up a sitcom each week."[4]

To others, however, it seemed that Ellen's show was focusing on humor that appealed to a gay audience rather than a more diverse one. Still others thought the writing had suffered. According to GLAAD, Stuart Bloomberg, chairman of ABC entertainment, stated that "as [*Ellen*] became more politicized and issue-oriented, it became less funny and audiences noticed." Through Chastity Bono and GLAAD's efforts, a vigorous letter-writing campaign called "Save Ellen!" was started.[5]

However, the television industry is a numbers game. and the *Ellen's* ratings were just too low. According to USC professor Charles Fleming, who teaches entertainment reporting, "The broadcast executives who program these shows, and the standards and practices geniuses who answer to them, and the writer-producers they employ are all doing nothing more than reflecting a conservative version of what the audience is telling them it likes."[6]

Unfortunately, no number of letter-writing campaigns could save the show. Almost one year to the day that Ellen Morgan came out of the closet, Ellen DeGeneres found out in the television trade journals that her show was canceled. Ellen Morgan would shut the door and say goodbye, and Ellen DeGeneres would say goodbye to television for quite some time. *Ellen* was canceled in April 1998. At the taping of the final episode, Ellen was tearful but thanked her staff and her cast for being part of a controversial show and for supporting her decision to come out, even through the hard times.

How did America respond to the show's cancellation? Again, it depends on who you ask. Naturally, conservative groups were pleased. Richard Land, head of the Southern Baptist Convention's Ethics and Religious Liberty Commission, said, "Ellen's insistence in giving a week-by-week, graphic depiction and description of the lead character's deviant sexual behavior has been rightly and roundly rejected by the American viewing public." Accuracy in Media praised the cancellation, while gay activists called Ellen's achievements historic.[7]

Ellen later told Sam Donaldson of ABC News that in retrospect, she could understand how the station was forced to cancel the show, and how, if she were in that position, she would have done the same thing. She said, "It's a very—there should have been a digestion process that I didn't take into consideration. I really expected everybody to open up their arms and say, 'We love you no matter what.' And, you know, that was—that was naive of me and I realize I would have liked a little more support and a little more help and just a gentler way of saying goodbye rather than reading it in the trades. But, you know, but I think anybody probably would have done the same thing."[8] With the benefit of hindsight over her nationally publicized coming out and the reactions that followed, Ellen reflected on the last year and realized that her career was changed because of the one thing she was trying to avoid—the fact that people seemed not to like her because she was gay.

Hollywood quickly moved on. On the next fall television schedule—only one season after *Ellen* had been canceled—NBC debuted a new comedy centered on the lives of a gay man (Will) and his best friend (Grace), on September 21, 1998. The sitcom starred Eric McCormack as Will, Debra Messing as Grace, Megan Mullally as Karen, and Sean Hayes as Jack. Later, the show included story lines on Jack (another flamboyantly gay man) and Karen (a straight and married wealthy woman who loves to indulge in shopping, booze, and pills). Cocreator Max Mutchnick described the transition from *Ellen* to *Will & Grace:* "*Ellen* was about the journey of that character. Ours is the celebration of this relationship. We're in broader, more appealing territory."[9] *Will & Grace* ran for eight successful seasons and won 16 Primetime Emmys and seven GLAAD Media Awards.

After the cancellation of *Ellen,* Ellen's relationship with Anne just wasn't the same as she struggled to rebound from the show's cancellation. Her career was taking a downturn, and even though she had a film credit to her name that year—as the voice of the dog in the 1998 film *Doctor Doolittle,* starring Eddie Murphy—which might have inspired her to press on career-wise, the normally bubbly, hard-working comedian was understandably depressed. She told Style.com that she was just so angry that she lost everything she had worked so hard for and found that magazines were now making her the punch line of the jokes, a type of comedy she tried so hard to avoid in her career.

Ellen's fantasy of how opinions and acceptance of homosexuality would change just didn't happen. To try and help overcome the dejection that she had been feeling, Ellen and Anne packed up and moved from the hustle and bustle of Hollywood to the smaller and more sedate Ojai, a city in Ventura County, California, situated in the Ojai Valley and surrounded by hills and mountains.

IN HONOR OF MATTHEW

Even though the gay community looked up to her after her own coming out, Ellen stressed that she didn't want to be a role model for the gay community. However, one tragic event made Ellen reconsider—if just for a little while. Matthew Shepard, a teen gay male, was murdered on October 7, 1998, lured out of a bar by two other 21-year-old young men, Aaron McKinney and Russell Henderson, on the pretext that they were gay as well. He was led to the woods, tied to a split-rail fence, pistol-whipped, beaten, and left for 18 hours in the cold of the night. He was found but later died in the hospital with his family by his side.[10]

Matthew's death became the hate crime attack heard around the world. There were reactions and protest demonstrations. Both men who killed Matthew received double life sentences in jail. Supporters of hate-crimes legislation worked with Congress to enact a law expanding federal penalties for acts of violence against homosexuals, named after Matthew, but to date no law has been passed to protect victims of hate crimes.

Antigay protestors rallied at Matthew's funeral holding signs that read, "Matt Shepard rots in hell" and other derogatory comments. Three films were made about or based on Matthew's story: *The Laramie Project* (2002); *Anatomy of a Hate Crime* (2001); and *The Matthew Shepard Story* (2002).

After both Ellen and Anne were devastated by Matthew's death, they made it a point to go to Washington, D.C., and talk to Congress in October 1998. Ellen told Congress that an attack like the one Matthew was subjected to was the exact thing she was trying to stop by coming out on national television: "When Matthew Shepard was killed, I don't know why, but I didn't think that would happen anymore. I thought people would be like, 'We love all gay people.' I know that sounds stupid. But I took it so personally when that happened to Matthew. It just was devastating to me that that could still go on."[11] Ellen would make another plea like this later in her career.

CAREER AND RELATIONSHIP CHANGE

For the next two years, the only acting or performing that Ellen did involved a few roles in major motion pictures. The first was opposite the mustachioed Tom Selleck in the 1999 romantic comedy *The Love Letter*. Ellen portrayed Janet Hall, and the movie centered on a mysterious love letter that everybody thinks is for them. The film received mixed reviews. Ellen was also cast as the cynical Sergeant Rita Pompano, who unravels a murder-for-insurance plot in the 1999 film *Goodbye Lover*, costarring Don Johnson, Dermot Mulroney, and Mary-Louise Parker. The film was described as "a tawdry, tasty film noir with a soft spot for its scheming antiheroine."[12]

She was also cast as Cynthia in Ron Howard's comedy film *EDtv*, a 1999 film about a video store clerk who agrees to have his life filmed by a camera crew for a TV network. Once again, critics adored

Ellen's performance but weren't so keen on the movie. The *San Francisco Chronicle* review said that *EDtv* generated some legitimate laughs. While Ellen's style of humor worked well in the movie, the supporting cast didn't hold water to Matthew McConaughey and Ellen, according to many reviews and reports.

At the prodding of Anne, Ellen kept busy with another film, HBO's *If These Walls Could Talk 2*, an intimate look at the American lesbian experience in the years 1961, 1972, and 2000. It was Anne's directorial debut, and she begged Ellen to participate. Anne directed the "2000" segment, a light-hearted story about a lesbian couple (portrayed by Sharon Stone and Ellen DeGeneres) trying to have a baby through artificial insemination. The segment included a love scene between the couple, although at first, Ellen resisted doing the scene. "She 'resisted, resisted, resisted,' says Heche. "I said, 'Come on, I've made out with some weasels, and I got you Sharon Stone!'"[13] Ellen eventually agreed to the love scenes (although there was no nudity involved) and also served as executive producer. She described the movie as everyone searching for the same things—love and acceptance. The show won Emmy Awards, Golden Globe Awards, Screen Actors Guild Awards, and NAACP awards.

Sadly, though, Anne and Ellen didn't last much longer as a couple. In 2000, after three and a half years together, they announced to the *New York Daily News* that they had indeed broken up. The couple called it an amicable split, but only hours after news of the split broke, in a strange twist, Anne was found wandering through a rural stretch of central California in Fresno. She was briefly hospitalized, and CNN reported that the 31-year-old actress appeared shaken and confused when she wandered up to a stranger's home. When asked about her breakdown, Anne said she was on the drug Ecstasy, a mood-elevating drug that produces a relaxed, euphoric state. She described herself as insane—even during the time of her relationship with Ellen. She also believed she was two people; one of her personalities was Celestia, whom Anne claimed was the daughter of God and half-sibling of Jesus, spoke a different language directly with God, and had contact with extraterrestrials.[14]

Anne's breakdown not only occurred at the time of her breakup with Ellen but also seemed to be timed perfectly to the release of her book *Call Me Crazy*. The book was a tell-all memoir in which the actress admitted that she was sexually abused by her father, Donald, from the time she was a toddler until she was 12. She also wrote that her father, who admitted that he was a gay man, died of AIDS in 1983. In the book, Anne explained how she created a fantasy world to live in when she was younger, called the Fourth Dimension, where she survived her abuse. Critic Lisa Schwarzbaum of *Entertainment Weekly* questioned why Anne wrote the book and lambasted her limited writing skills.

Ellen found herself in an interesting position—her girlfriend, who had pushed her to be more public about her homosexuality, had left and claimed to have been crazy when she was with Ellen. Ironically, Anne married cameraman Coleman Laffoon the following year.

Ellen's show was cancelled, and her stand-up career was at a standstill. All Ellen wanted was for everyone to stop focusing on her social life and start focusing on her as a performer. "It hurt me as a performer because I had worked so hard to get to a certain point and now here I am just trying to get back to that point and erase everything else and say, forget about all that stuff and please just focus on me as a comedian," she said.[15] Ellen realized that it was time for her to put her life back together piece by piece.

NOTES

1. John Gallagher, "Ellen DeGeneres: 'We're Not Coming Back,'" *The Advocate*, April 14, 1998.

2. http://www.planetout.com/entertainment/news/?sernum=168.

3. John Gallagher, "Ellen DeGeneres: 'We're Not Coming Back.'"

4. John Gallagher, "Ellen DeGeneres: 'We're Not Coming Back.'"

5. "Jerry-Rigged." *EW* Online, March 25, 1994.

6. http://www.usc.edu/student-affairs/dt/V142/N56/12-gayles.56d.html.

7. http://findarticles.com/p/articles/mi_m1589/is_n761/ai_20752204.

8. http://www.allbusiness.com/population-demographics/demographic-groups-gays-lesbians/6451421–1.html.

9. http://www.glaad.org/media/resource_kit_detail.php?id=4000.

10. http://www.matthewshepard.org/site/PageServer?pagename=Press_Media_Releases_Main_Page.

11. http://www.planetout.com/entertainment/news/?sernum=168.

12. http://www.thedavidlawrenceshow.com/mary_louise_parker_005545.html.

13. Gail Shister, "Intimate Portrait," *The Record* (New Jersey), All Editions, sec. Your Time, Y1, February 2, 2000.

14. http://www.usatoday.com/life/2001–09–04-heche.htm.

15. http://www.ellen-forum.de/ellen/presse/sandiegounion.html.

Ellen started off her career doing stand-up comedy performances in the 1980s. Photofest.

One of Ellen's first television roles was on the short-lived sitcom Open House (Fox) in 1989. Fox/Photofest.

In "The Puppy Episode" airing on April 30, 1997, on Ellen, *character Ellen Morgan announces she's gay. Ellen DeGeneres made the same announcement that year as well. ABC/Photofest.*

Ellen DeGeneres, host of the 53rd Annual Primetime Emmy Awards in 2001, appeared on stage in a costume similar to that worn by pop singer Bjork at the Oscar Awards. AP Photo/Kevork Djansezian.

Jennifer Aniston is a guest on the season premiere of the daytime talk show The Ellen DeGeneres Show *on September 8, 2003. The show has gone on to win numerous awards and has sent Ellen's career skyrocketing once again. Telepictures/Photofest.*

Ellen DeGeneres arrives at the 19th Annual GLAAD Media Awards on Saturday, April 26, 2008, in the Hollywood section of Los Angeles. DeGeneres is putting the state Supreme Court ruling in favor of gay marriage into action—she and actress Portia de Rossi wed on August 16, 2008 at their home in Beverly Hills, California. AP Photo/Chris Weeks.

Chapter 7

BOUNCING BACK

But seriously, I think overall in the scheme of things winning an Emmy is not important. Let's get our priorities straight. I think we all know what's really important in life—winning an Oscar.

—*Ellen DeGeneres*

Although Ellen had broken up with Anne Heche, she began to bounce back, at least where her love life was concerned. Through mutual friends, she met Alexandra Hedison, a former actress turned photographer and the daughter of Bridget and Albert David Hedison, a noted soap star who was seen on *Another World* and *The Young and the Restless* in the 1960s. In an interview for *Artworks* magazine, Alexandra says that she knew she was gay in high school but—like Ellen—didn't reveal her sexuality until she was 18.

Alexandra made an attempt at acting, appearing in bit parts on various television shows including *Silk Stalkings, Melrose Place, Lois & Clark,* and *Diagnosis Murder.* However, she says she was unhappy with acting as a career choice, even though she was supporting herself as a working actress.

After Alexandra was given her first camera as a gift from her father, she found what she considered to be her true passion—photography—and began a new career. She put acting on hold (although she did resume acting part time in 2006 when she appeared in *The L Word* as the character Dylan Moreland for eight episodes). Ellen and Alexandra started dating and made their first public appearance at a breast-cancer fund-raiser. Within the year, Ellen and Alexandra were cohabitating, and Ellen expressed her love for Alexandra in an interview with *The Advocate*, calling her an amazing person who is really grounded and healthy. Alexandra found Ellen to be a loving and supportive partner, especially when it came to her budding photography career. Ellen even helped to promote Alexandra's photography exhibits and encouraged her to hang her photographs at home.

Ellen's mother was happy for her, especially after Ellen's extremely public coming out and relationship with Heche. Ellen's mother, Betty, reportedly said, "She [Hedison] is no mystery. I've met her a couple times, and she's a lovely, lovely person. She has a great sense of humor, which Ellen can certainly appreciate...As a mother, I'm just happy to see my child happy. So much has happened to Ellen, she's been so devastated. As a mother, it's so difficult. When your child hurts, you hurt, too. You just feel so helpless."[1]

Ellen didn't give up on her comeback, and it didn't take much longer to make it. She turned to her roots, her one comfort zone—stand-up comedy—and hit the road again, performing in various venues, such as the Beacon Theater in Manhattan. Ellen often credited the power of positive thinking for her rebirth. Positive thinking is a mental attitude that convinces the individual that they are expecting something good and favorable from every situation.

The power of positive thinking came from a book that Ellen read during her downtime—*The Four Agreements: A Practical Guide to Personal Freedom, A Toltec Wisdom Book* (1997) by author Don Miguel Ruiz, a book based on ancient Toltec wisdom. Ruiz provides four agreements that he says can rapidly transform our lives to a new experience of freedom, true happiness, and love. The Four Agreements are: Be Impeccable with Your Word, Don't Take Anything Personally, Don't Make Assumptions, Always Do Your Best.

Ruiz also wrote *The Mastery of Love: A Practical Guide to the Art of Relationship* (2002) and *Beyond Fear: A Toltec Guide to Freedom and Joy* (1997). Ellen recommended *The Four Agreements* to Oprah Winfrey when she appeared on her show in October 2001, and she got the opportunity to interview Ruiz, gushing about his book and the changes that she experienced after she read it. During the interview with Ruiz, Ellen asked him about the first agreement, which states that it's important to be impeccable with your word, and wondered why everybody loves gossip and how most people live their life for an end result. This hit home with Ellen and helped her to face the next part of her life.

A TRIUMPHANT RETURN

From this point forward, Ellen danced her way to the top—both literally and figuratively. On July 23, 2000, she made her triumphant return to cable television to perform her HBO Comedy Special, *Ellen DeGeneres: The Beginning*, a one-hour stand-up performance where Ellen expounds on everything from fashion to friends. It was a hit and was nominated for two Primetime Emmy Awards, including Outstanding Individual Performance in a Variety or Music Program and Outstanding Variety, Music or Comedy Special. Ellen didn't win, but she continued on her path back to success.

When she was interviewed a few years later by Barbara Walters, Ellen explained that she decided to write that special specifically so that she could turn her floundering career around: "They'll see that I'm funny, and you know, I'll get a job." She might have been joking around, but once again—like the time she envisioned performing the "Phone Call to God" on the *Tonight Show*—she was right. Thanks to her rousing cable success, the television industry called Ellen back—to a new station with a new sitcom and an invitation to host the *53rd Annual Primetime Emmy Awards* on CBS in September.

Her new half-hour sitcom, *The Ellen Show*, premiered on CBS in September 2001. Ellen played an Internet executive, who—yes—was a lesbian and was returning to her hometown for a quieter way of life. This show was meant to be a lighter sitcom than her last show, with legendary comedienne Cloris Leachman cast as Ellen's mother. Although Ellen's character was gay, there were only a few allusions to that fact. The show was originally scheduled for Friday nights at 8 P.M., making it more appropriate for the family viewing hour. This was a definite switch from the parental warnings her previous sitcom was given.

"It wasn't even an issue when I said my character's going to be gay—that was sort of a given," says Ellen. "But the whole deal is, I did

12 to 15 years of stand-up before I did (*Ellen*). Granted, I was not out, but none of my material ever came from dating. It was all just situations and life issues. And this time around, I'm just trying to do a funny show."[2] Funny, but with hardly any reflection on the character's sexuality, according to Jennifer Reed, contributor to *Queer Popular Culture: Literature, Media, Film and Television*. Reed wrote, "In this new incarnation, DeGeneres so desexualized herself, so depoliticized herself that she evacuated the cultural space she created with *Ellen*. *The Ellen Show* brings the lesbian home and puts her right back in her place." Reed didn't necessarily think that was a good thing.

The author also discussed how Ellen tried to "normalize" a gay person in a straight person's world: "DeGeneres was fairly straightforward about replacing sexuality with place—urban versus small town—as a marker of difference." Ellen said that her new character would not have a love life, deeming it "not necessary," since many story lines are often themed around life issues other than dating. Ellen compared her show to the *Andy Griffith Show*, which was based more around the characters in the town and the situations they found themselves in than their personal lives. Sadly, America might also not have been ready for funny by the time Ellen's new sitcom debuted.

On September 11, 2001, by approximately 9 A.M., life in America drastically changed. A series of coordinated suicide attacks by the terrorist group al-Qaeda hit the United States. Four commercial airliners were hijacked. Two of the airliners were plunged into the World Trade Center in New York City right at the time of the hustle and bustle of the morning commute. One airplane was crashed into the Pentagon in Washington, D.C., and the final jet crashed in a field outside of Pennsylvania. The two World Trade Center buildings ultimately collapsed, and almost three thousand people—including the hijackers—perished that day.

In just five days, Ellen was scheduled to host the *53rd Annual Primetime Emmy Awards* on CBS, but due to the heartbreaking circumstances, they were postponed. In the meantime, the debut of Ellen's new show also wasn't going well. Perhaps it was just bad timing and American audiences were not ready for laughs, but *The Ellen Show* was cancelled after only 13 episodes. In the meantime, CBS wanted to reschedule the Emmy Awards for an October broadcast, but due to America's retaliatory attack on Afghanistan, the show was postponed again. Finally, after two attempts, producers decided that the show would finally be broadcast on Sunday, November 4, 2001, almost two months after the devastating tragedy that shook the nation.

Hosting this particular Emmy Awards was going to be a tough gig for Ellen, who remained committed to hosting the ceremony. Trying to make America laugh after just going through one of the worst tragedies the country had ever seen seemed like an impossible task. How would Ellen manage? In her opening monologue, Ellen joked, "We're told to go on living our lives as usual, because to do otherwise is to let the terrorists win, and really, what would upset the Taliban more than a gay woman wearing a suit in front of a room full of Jews?"

Even under the gloomy circumstances, Ellen rocked the event. For a few brief hours, Americans' minds were removed from the heart-wrenching events and focused on simple entertainment. *TV Guide* Online said that "from the moment that she was called to the plate by Walter Cronkite (appearing via satellite), the host hit one home run after another. Whether paying lip service to Emmy's all-American timeslot competitor, the World Series; making boss Les Moonves squirm by bringing up the future of her struggling series, *The Ellen Show*; or ignoring Steve Martin (Anne Heche's ex) to interview a seat filler, then introducing Martin as Leslie Nielsen, the funny lady distinguished herself not just as the night's MVP, but as one of the industry's."[3] Ellen's hosting style was widely praised, and she would return to host again in 2005.

2003—SHE'S BAAAACKK!

Throughout 2002, Ellen continued performing stand-up to rave reviews. Bruce Weber of the *New York Times*, after witnessing Ellen's one-night-only show at the Avery Fisher Hall at Lincoln Center, said, "It felt as if Ms. DeGeneres were living comfortably in her own skin rather than wrapping herself itchily in ours."[4] Weber was right. Ellen was very comfortable where she was, and in the next year, she would climb back on the top of the Hollywood heap where it seemed that she could do no wrong. She had finally landed a part in a blockbuster movie—and nobody would even see her on the screen.

For Ellen, it was the year of the fish. According to Pixar, *Finding Nemo* was a computer-animated underwater adventure of a father fish that is separated from his son and must embark on an epic journey to bring him back home. Ellen was wooed, or approached, by Andrew Stanton, a writer and director at Pixar, for the role of Dory. Ellen says she was a bit confused when first approached. "He told me it was this motor-mouthed fish with memory loss. I wondered what exactly it was in me that had inspired the character. I warned him I might just forget I'd committed to the project if I didn't like what he'd written," she quipped.[5]

But she did commit to the project, and she enjoyed every minute of it: "It was fun to play, because I got to go in, over the course of three years, and stand there and play this happy, optimistic, hopeful, fearless creature every time I was [recording Dory's voice]. Then, I'd go in my car, and I'd go home and get disappointed by people."[6] As a stand-up comic, Ellen found the actual recording of her voice-over to be rather difficult because in a cartoon—unlike the modus operandi of most stand-up comedians—there is no ability to show facial expressions or body movement. Ellen had to make the character come alive with only one instrument—her voice. She did it well, and *Finding Nemo* became the movie hit that Ellen was waiting for. The G-rated film went on to gross over $864 million worldwide and sold more than 40 million DVD copies as of 2006. It received two Chicago Film Critics Association Awards—one for Best Picture—and Ellen received an award for Best Supporting Actress. The Nickelodeon Kids Choice Awards also voted *Finding Nemo* their favorite movie that year and voted Ellen the favorite voice from an animated movie.

ON THE ROAD AGAIN

Ellen was ready to hit the road again, and she took her stand-up act on a cross-country 35-city comedy tour entitled *Here and Now, Modern Life and Other Inconveniences*, which was taped for HBO. As Ellen describes, going on tour at this point might have been for medicinal purposes: "I thought, why should I pay a stranger to listen to me talk when I can get strangers to pay to listen to me talk? That's when I came up with the idea of touring." The show concluded with a performance that she did at the Beacon Theater in New York, which scored higher than any previous HBO Comedy Special. Ellen was nominated for two Primetime Emmys for this tour.[7]

"'It does feel like a comeback to me," says the comedian, who was 42 years old. "Some people don't look at it as a comeback because it doesn't seem like I went anywhere. But I did go somewhere. I went pretty far down. I was in a depression for a pretty long time."[8]

Proud of herself for taking that first step and returning to her stand-up roots, Ellen realized that there were going to be repercussions, including a loss of part of her fan base. "Everybody's going to want something different from me at this point. There'll be people who will be upset if I say one little thing. People who just want me to get up and be political will be upset because I'm not being political on stage, but I never have been. I started writing that kind of stuff, but it didn't feel right," she says.[9]

TALK, TALK, TALK...AND DANCE

In 2003, things were getting better and better and bigger and bigger for the comedian. On September 8, 2003, Ellen DeGeneres once again returned to television as host of her own daytime talk show, *The Ellen DeGeneres Show*, and once again, the question was raised as to whether Ellen would focus on gay themes. "It's hard because until I'm on the air, I think it's this big question," she told the *New York Daily News* before the talk show's debut. Because people for some reason think, "of course to the show is going to be about [being gay]. It's really got nothing to do with the show. People know I'm gay, there's no surprise there, I'm not hiding anything. And the stuff people keep focusing on is five years old. It's like, at some point, I hope it goes away."[10]

Thankfully, for quite some time it did just that. It went away. Ellen had a place on television. A place to be who she wanted to be and make people laugh the way she wanted to make people laugh. What Ellen wanted was a fun show, and that's exactly what *The Ellen DeGeneres Show* was. "You know, the biggest difference is I get to be myself—even though I don't really think I've been hiding behind a character so much in my last two shows," she says. "But I get to be myself and I get to think on my feet and talk to people and have something new and interesting every single day. On a sitcom, the world is what it is—different crappy situations that the writers come up with—and it's a character and not quite me. This is more about being able to be myself."[11]

She also had a team of writers, a disc jockey named Tony Okungbowa, and a place to make people laugh and dance, which she does before tapings, after her monologue, and during commercial breaks. "If I don't dance, they're feeling left out," says Ellen. "They want to dance now. I'm stuck. I'm waiting for it to be a *Saturday Night Live* parody. I know to some people it's idiotic. A lot of people really love it. I do love it."[12]

And so did everyone else. Fellow comedian and host of *The Tonight Show*, Jay Leno, knew Ellen would be back even after everything she had been through.

Writer Stephen Kelly of PopMatters.com said her show had a "pleasant, cheery feel…DeGeneres evinces no interest in being edgy or even especially passionate about political or social issues. Genial as she is, invites us to kick up our feet and relax."[13] A few years later, her decision to remain politically neutral would change, but for now—in its freshman year—*The Ellen DeGeneres Show* won four daytime Emmys out of 12 nominations, including outstanding talk show.

Ellen premiered her season with a who's who of A-listers, including Jennifer Aniston, Justin Timberlake, Macy Gray, and John Travolta. Ellen also returned to writing, and in October 2003, her second book, *The Funny Thing Is…* was published and made the *New York Times* bestseller list. Ellen's career had a golden touch, and her relationship with Alexandra was doing just fine, thank you. Then along came Portia.

PORTIA DE ROSSI

Even though they had publicly proclaimed their love for each other, the relationship between Alexandra and Ellen would not last much longer. When Ellen arrived for a photo shoot in early 2004, she met the young and beautiful Portia de Rossi.

Portia de Rossi was born on January 31, 1973, in Melbourne, Australia, but at that time was known as Amanda Lee Rogers. She changed her name to the more glamorous Portia de Rossi when she was 15 years old. A tall, leggy blonde, Portia says she changed her name legally because it was a connection to her struggle about being gay. Everything in her life didn't fit, so she attempted to change and identify those things that did. As a result, she started with her name and changed it to Portia because, as a Shakespeare fan, she chose to name herself after her namesake in *The Merchant of Venice*. She chose De Rossi as her surname because, as an Australian, she was attracted to the exotic Italian name and felt that it suited her personality more than her birth name.

Portia was raised by her mother, Margaret, and her father, Barry Rodgers, who is reported to have died in 1982.[14] As a child, Portia modeled but planned on majoring in law when she got older. She attended Melbourne University, but was soon bitten by the acting bug. In her first role, in the Australian film *Sirens,* which starred Hugh Grant, Portia portrayed a maid turned model. Following the release of this film, Portia—in a similar move that Ellen made when she wanted to hit it big—relocated to Los Angeles to pursue her Hollywood dreams. At this point in her career, she was considered a beautiful and heterosexual starlet, and she was even married for a brief period of time to documentary filmmaker Mel Metcalfe. But Hollywood had yet to learn that Portia de Rossi was gay.

Portia kicked off her career quickly and guest starred on several television shows before earning a role in the parody film *Scream 2.* But it was the legal drama *Ally McBeal* on the Fox network, and her character Nelle Porter, a lawyer and resident vixen, that put Portia on Hollywood's radar screen.

Although her career was going well, Portia also struggled with a few obstacles in her personal life. She suffered from anorexia— anorexia is an eating disorder where people starve themselves— during her days on *Ally McBeal*. While penning an article for *People* magazine on her recovery, Portia explained how it was a good opportunity for her to say, 'Do as I say, not as I do.' After her personal experience in Hollywood, Portia knew how tough the industry could be on body image and wanted to set a positive example after having some bad body habits of her own. She also explained how she would live on 300 calories a day and Jello while overdoing the exercise program. Soon, she was a mere 82 pounds, and it was her mother and brother in Australia who told her she would die if she didn't change what she was doing.

At the same time, Portia was very concerned about the impact that the revelation of her sexuality would have on her acting and modeling career and her continued acceptance in Hollywood. Her appearances on *Ally McBeal* not only catapulted her career but also put her in the public spotlight—again similar to what Ellen experienced when her sitcom propelled her to Hollywood's A-list. In an interview with *The Advocate*, Portia explained how she finally, and unexpectedly, decided to become open about the fact that she was gay after her *Ally McBeal* castmate, Greg Germann, confronted her and guessed correctly about her sexuality.

"I'd been on the show for about two months," she said, "before we had to go to New York to do press, and Greg Germann and I were talking in the bar one night and he said, 'There's something about you I can't quite put my finger on... Are you gay?' Of course, I stammered and stuttered, and looked at the ground and went, 'Uh...uh...uh...maybe, I don't know. I think so. I'm not sure.' He looked at me and said, 'Have you struggled with it...?' That was so profound." In 2001, Portia went public with her romance with Francesca Gregorini, daughter of Beatles sensation Ringo Starr, and realized that now that everyone knew about her homosexuality, there was no turning back. While that might scare others who have come out of the closet, Portia felt relief.

Then in 2001, Portia starred in the movie *Who Is Cletis Tout?* with comedian Tim Allen and Christian Slater, in which she portrayed Tess Tobias. Portia's film and television career was going well, but now that she had gone public as a lesbian, the paparazzi chased down Portia and Francesca and splashed their romance all over the tabloids. Portia has been described as a quiet woman who desires to keep out of the limelight when she is not working, and this was difficult to handle.

"It sounds so trite, but my private life is mine," Portia told an Australian newspaper. "When you have the paparazzi hiding in the bushes outside your home, about the only thing you can control is how you respond publicly. When I hear celebrities talking about their marriages or other things that are intensely personal, I cringe. I just think, 'Keep it to yourself.' It's like desperate attention-seeking."[15]

While Portia was immersed in her career and in an open relationship with Francesca—she even tattooed Francesca's initials on her hand—Ellen was deep in the throes of a relationship with Alexandra and confessed her love publicly. But when Ellen and Portia met at a photo shoot in early 2004, it was hard to deny the attraction between the two women. Portia even admitted that when she first saw Ellen, "she took my breath away." However, since both women were currently in long-term relationships, they didn't pursue their attraction at that time.

According to the *New York Post's* Page Six column, Portia was familiar with Ellen's public outing, and she admired how Ellen fought back in the face of adversity: "When I watched Ellen come out in '97, my jaw was on the floor. I thought, there are some people who break the doors down, hold them open and some people who walk right through. I always thought I was the latter. Thanks so much, everybody, thanks for making gay marriage legal, thank you for everything you've done. I'm just going to walk through that door."[16]

At the end of the year, on December 1, 2004, at the Shrine Auditorium in Los Angeles, Ellen and Portia met up again for the VH-1 Big '04 awards, and this time, couldn't deny their attraction. So they both decided to terminate their current relationships and begin dating. In December 2004, Alexandra and Ellen called it quits, and Alexandra moved out of the Hollywood home that she shared with Ellen.

"I could say the same thing I've said in every relationship: 'I'm happy.' But there's happiness and there's love, and then there's completion," said Ellen. "It doesn't take away from any of the relationships that I've had, 'cause I've had amazing relationships.... But I feel like I found my perfect fit."[17]

Even though Hollywood and the rest of the world seemed to know about their relationship, Portia still had to tell one more person—her grandmother—that she was gay and in a relationship with Ellen. In an interview with *The Advocate,* she explained how she had a warm conversation with her grandmother and told her that she was in love. When her grandmother asked, "What's his name?" Portia responded "Ellen DeGeneres." Her grandmother responded by saying, "Well this is a very bad day. Darlin', you're not

one of those." Fortunately for Portia, her grandmother's denounce-
ment of her relationship lasted only two minutes and ended when
her grandmother held her arms out and said, "I love you just the
same."[18]

When Ellen and Portia went public, the paparazzi were once
again fascinated with the relationship. The *Chicago Sun Times* even
went as far as interviewing an author to read the couple's body language toward each other. The author said, "They have the body
language of one of the most in-love couples you will ever have the
privilege of meeting," she says. "They practically melt into each
other, as though they were one body."[19]

Unfortunately, jilted lover Alexandra wasn't taking the breakup
so well and even met with lawyers to determine if she had enough
evidence to file a palimony suit against Ellen. Palimony is a form
of alimony—monetary damages—awarded to one of the partners in
a romantic relationship after the breakup of that relationship following a long period of living together. Hedison was also rumored
to be filing suit against Portia, claiming "alienation of affection," a
lawsuit in which a spouse can sue a third party (in this case Portia)
if her partner leaves the relationship for another person. There was
no evidence that the lawsuit went forward.[20]

SELLING SUCCESS

In season two, *The Ellen DeGeneres Show* won five daytime
Emmys, and what often begins to happen when you become successful on television is that people want you to start selling their
merchandise. In 2004, one of Ellen's childhood dreams came true
when she became the first openly gay person chosen to represent
American Express in its new "My life. My card." campaign. According to the *Hollywood Reporter*, Ellen was actually instrumental
in developing the concept for her spot, in which she appears in her
office and on the set of her show with a turtle, elephant, kangaroo,
and other animals as her colleagues: "The inspiration came from
Amex's Questionnaire print campaign in which its celebrity endors-
ers supplied answers to some personal questions. In hers, DeGeneres
wrote that working with animals was her childhood ambition."[21]
She told *TV Week* that it's okay to do some selling if it's something

that makes sense to her, such as the American Express commercial that she did in 2004.

Another paparazzi and fan obsession that comes along with celebrity is the illustrious red carpet, where celebrities are asked who designed their dresses and tuxedos. Only once had Ellen donned an elegant dress—when she cohosted the 1994 Primetime Emmy Awards with Patricia Richardson. After that, she chose to dress in what made her most comfortable, and for Ellen, that was softer tuxedos rather than formal dresses. Portia, however, always dressed in glamorous long gowns. But Ellen didn't avoid a dress for the entire night at the Emmys. In her typical comical style, the crowd finally got a chance to see Ellen wear a dress—one with a large swan wrapped around her neck, mimicking a similar frock once worn to the Oscars by the singer Björk.

"I had written two other totally different monologues," Ellen said. "And it could have been morose. But it was still important to wear the Bjork swan dress to try to lighten it up. We didn't want to be disrespectful, but we still wanted to celebrate people's hard work and people wanted to laugh. So I was very proud that it turned out the way it did."[22]

AND THE OSCAR GOES TO...

Ellen received rave reviews for her cohosting duties, and she also realized that she enjoyed her hosting duties. She decided that she wanted to host another, bigger awards show—and there's nothing bigger in Hollywood than the Academy Awards, also known as the Oscars. In 2005, that ambition of hers came true when she was asked to host the *79th Annual Academy Awards*, following in the footsteps of such legendary hosts as Bob Hope, Johnny Carson, Billy Crystal, Danny Kaye, and Whoopi Goldberg. Ellen would be the first openly gay entertainer to host the Academy Awards.

"She just sparkles," said Academy President Sid Ganis. "She is such a pleasure to watch. Her wit cuts to the truth of things, but in a wonderfully warm-spirited way. I think she'll be a fantastic host for this show and we're extremely pleased that she's agreed to do it."[23] Laura Ziskin, producer of the Academy Awards, said, "Ellen De-

Generes was born to host the Academy Awards. There is no more challenging hosting job in show business. It requires someone who can keep the show alive and fresh and moving, as well as someone who is a flat-out great entertainer. Ellen completely fits the bill. I can already tell she is going to set the bar very high for herself and therefore for all of us involved in putting on the show. Now all we need is a lot of great movies."[24]

When Laura Ziskin called, Ellen was thrilled. "There's two things I've always wanted to do in my life. One is to host the Oscars. The second is to get a call from Laura Ziskin. You can imagine that day's diary entry," said Ellen. She had wanted to host the Oscars for quite some time and hoped that the producers would ask her: "I'd actually turned down the Emmys a couple years in a row after [hosting the post-9/11 telecast] because I wanted to do the Oscars and then finally I was like [*sigh*], 'It's not happening, so I'll just host the Emmys again.'"[25]

But once again, in what seemed to be an unfortunate pattern of events, Ellen's hosting duties were put to the test when the ceremony was scheduled only a few weeks after the catastrophic Hurricane Katrina hit her hometown of New Orleans, Louisiana. Ellen was hoping that the hosting duties were still hers, so she told the executive producer that it was important now to make people laugh, without forgetting about the events that had just taken place. She started making people laugh before she even hit the stage. Ellen jokingly told *Entertainment Weekly* that her one good-luck ritual she had before walking out to host the Oscars is "I like to rub mayonnaise on my thighs...It's not so much a ritual—it's just how I get pants on, now that I think about it."[26]

After the event, Ellen broke down and explained, "I'm crying for many reasons. I'm tired, so I'm emotional...[but hosting the Oscars] represented so many things to me. It represented that people believed in me, they took a chance in me to hold something like that together, that people would want to see me."[27]

The *Hollywood Reporter* critiqued Ellen's performance, saying that "while Ellen DeGeneres didn't ruffle any feathers the way previous hosts have done, she also didn't deliver the kind of big laughs that Oscar audiences got once upon a time from hosts like Bob Hope,

Johnny Carson and Billy Crystal. Those guys knew exactly how to skewer the stars sitting before them and how to get away with it. They understood how far they could push the envelope to get a laugh, but not to draw blood." The critic said that Ellen didn't deliver the kind of topical references that would have drawn big laughs.[28] In the end, Ellen was nominated for an Emmy Award as host of the Academy Awards broadcast, and Laura Ziskin said the results were spectacular. "She's a good human and that comes across, so people relax and feel comfortable," said Ziskin. "She's so game, and I had a spectacular time working with her. What more could you ask for?"[29]

Ellen was now enjoying tremendous success in all venues. In 2005, she won a Grammy Award for Best Comedy Album for the audio version of her book. That same year, *The Ellen DeGeneres Show* won five Daytime Emmy Awards, including best talk show host. Ellen repeated that win the following year when *The Ellen DeGeneres Show* won numerous Daytime Emmys, including Ellen's second consecutive Daytime Emmy for Outstanding Talk Show Host, Outstanding Talk Show, and Outstanding Special Class Writing. The show also won multiple People's Choice Awards, including Favorite Daytime Talk Show Host and People's Choice Awards Favorite Funny Female Star, again repeating her victories from a year earlier.

Ellen was supposed to team with her brother, Vance, to create a half-hour comedy pilot script based on a family and its pets, which Ellen said was a dream of theirs. "Over the years, we've talked about creating something together, but it didn't work out until now with the WB," said Vance. "Although she's a big star, Ellen is also my younger sister and you know what that means; our mom settles any creative arguments. Mom is tough, but fair. And she makes us soup."[30]

In 1999, Vance had been working as a correspondent for *The Daily Show* with Jon Stewart for over two years and on *The Late, Late Show* with Craig Ferguson. Behind the camera, he produced many shows, including *Pat Croce: Moving In*, was a staff writer on *Ellen*, and was a writer on the Grammy Award shows and on several Emmy Award shows.

NOTES

1. Hallie Levine, "Mom Shares Ellen's Joy—New Gal Pal Eases Pain of Heche Split," *New York Post*, October 24, 2000, sec. News, p. 15.

2. www.TVguideonline.com, August 16, 2001.

3. http://www.tvguide.com/News-Views/Interviews-Features/Article/default.aspx?posting={64D8D504–866F-42E9–81FD-D2A3868BE7B2.

4. http://query.nytimes.com/gst/fullpage.html?res=980CE0DF123FF9 32A15755C0A9649C8B63&sec=&spon=&pagewanted=all.

5. http://www.jam.canoe.ca/movies/artists/d/degeneres_ellen/2003/06/08.

6. tvguide.com/news-views/interviews-features/article/default.aspx?posting=(05D24875-F023–4C65-A883-D43A930B5185).

7. www.query.nytimes.com/gst/fullpage.html?res+980CE0DF123FF99.

8. "Ellen DeGeneres: The Beginning," Endnote: *Press-Telegram* (Long Beach, CA), AM, sec. Lifestyle, C1, June 21, 2000.

9. *Press-Telegram* (Long Beach, CA), AM, Lifestyle, C1, June 21, 2000.

10. www.stephenkellysf.com/tvreviews/ellen_degeneres.html.

11. Chris Rose, "Melancholy Ellen," *The Times-Picayune* (New Orleans, LA), sec. Living, p. 01, February 11, 2003.

12. *The New Orleans Times Picayune*, p. 08, May 16, 2004.

13. http://www.popmatters.com/com/tv/reviews/e/ellen-degeneres-show.shtml.

14. http://www.superiorpics.com/portia_de_rossi/.

15. http://www.afterellen.com/archive/ellen/People/portia2.html.

16. http://www.advocate.com/issue_story_ektid20037.asp.

17. http://www.people.com/people/article/0,,20009962,00.html.

18. Michele Kort, "Portia Heart & Soul," *The Advocate*, September 13, 2005.

19. *Chicago Sun-Times*, final edition, sec. Fluff, p. 08, May 28, 2006.

20. Bill Zwecker, "Ex Might Sue Ellen—and the Sitcom Star She's With," *Chicago Sun-Times*, sec. Features, p. 36, January 11, 2005.

21. http://www.hollywoodreporter.com/hr/content_display/news/e3i5-caaebc3b67867e5b00ffcaf1e20c6e5.

22. http://www.tvweek.com/news/2008/01/winning_way_with_awards_shows.php.

23. http://www.oscars.org/79academyawards/host.html.

24. http://www.oscars.org/79academyawards/host.html.

25. http://www.ew.com/ew/article/0,,20007870_20007899_20009762, 00.html.

26. http://www.ew.com/ew/article/0,,20009762,00.html.

27. http://www.people.com/people/package/redcarpet2007/article/ 0,,20006775_20013491,00.html.

28. http://www.hollywoodreporter.com/hr/content_display/news/e3i52 88266eb2bb5933f21f4783061e67d0.

29. http://www.tvweek.com/news/2008/01/winning_way_with_awards_ shows.php.

30. http://blogs.kansascity.com/tvbarn/2006/01/aka_the_vance_d.html.

Chapter 8

JUST KEEP DANCING

Oh, they're buzzin' around like bees to a honeycomb, aren't they?
I don't know what made me the special guest today. When other
people aren't available, I'm here. I'm the designated lesbian.

—*Ellen DeGeneres jokes to* TV Guide Online[1]

From 1997 to 2007, many changes took place in Ellen DeGeneres'
personal and professional lives. She made the most daring move to
announce her sexuality to America from the cover of a national
magazine. She took her television show persona on this journey
as well. They both came out of the closet together while millions
watched, but both Ellens weren't the only ones who took this cou-
rageous step. Ellen's valor undoubtedly helped countless other gay
people—celebrities and noncelebrities. On January 17, 2007, *Grey's
Anatomy* actor T. R. Knight appeared on *The Ellen DeGeneres Show*
as a guest and talked about his experiences during his own coming
out. During the interview, he credited Ellen for paving the way for
others to come out as well.

It was only fitting that in April 2007, GLAAD celebrated the
landmark 10-year anniversary of both Ellens' coming out. "Ellen
coming out ten years ago kicked off a tremendous decade of visibility for lesbian, gay, bisexual and transgender people," says GLAAD
President Neil G. Giuliano. "Ellen opened the closet door for
shows like *Will & Grace*, *The L Word* and *Ugly Betty* to succeed,

and for other out performers to live their lives openly and honestly. We know that with this kind of visibility comes understanding and acceptance."[2]

To mark the 10th anniversary of *Ellen's* historic "The Puppy Episode," the Oxygen network aired an *Ellen* marathon, reairing the two-part historic episode. In September 2007, *The Advocate*, which celebrated their 40th anniversary, voted Ellen to be their number one hero of the past 40 years.[3] And 10 years later, Ellen welcomed actress Laura Dern to *The Ellen DeGeneres Show*. Laura, now 40, portrayed Ellen's love interest Susan on *Ellen*. Laura revealed to Ellen that she had suffered her own surprisingly critical backlash in her career for playing Ellen's girlfriend and sharing an on-screen kiss with her. This renowned actress told Ellen that she couldn't get an acting job for more than a year after the episode had aired. Ellen was not aware of the fact that Laura had been snubbed by Hollywood and graciously apologized. "There was certainly backlash, I guess, we all felt from it," said Laura. Laura recovered career-wise and went on to star in many successful movies including *Jurassic Park*, *I Am Sam*, and *Year of the Dog*.

Interestingly enough, even talk show host Oprah Winfrey suffered from backlash after appearing as Ellen's therapist. The rumor mill was flooded with rumors that Oprah would be the next person to come out of the closet. The gossip persisted so much so that Oprah was forced to release a press release in which she denied any connection to being a homosexual and stated that she took the role on Ellen's sitcom simply to support her friend.

LOOK WHAT YOU DID

Call it coincidence, riding the wave, or pure inspiration, but whatever you call it, the Hollywood industry—especially television—saw a great deal of change with dramas and sitcoms introducing more gay characters after both Ellens proclaimed their sexuality to the world. There was also the creation of many gay-based television shows, such as *Queer Eye for the Straight Guy*.

"I think there needs to be a lot more of everything on television—not just lesbians," said Ellen to *Planet Out*. "I think the world is not accurately reflected.... But I think it's easier for people to accept gay men. People seem to feel a little more comfortable with gay men because they feel like they've always known them. We've always had people like Paul Lynde on *Hollywood Squares*, people that didn't necessarily come out and tell us they were gay, but it was obvious that they were. And gay men are fun and funny and witty, and lesbians don't have that kind of—that's not what we know them for. You and I are funny. We know that."[4]

GLAAD kept a running log of the changes that took place in Hollywood "after *Ellen*," as they call it. According to GLAAD.[5]

- In December 2000, life partners and co-producers Daniel Lipman and Ron Cowen adapt the hit British series *Queer as Folk* as a Showtime series for American audiences. Their goal is to present an honest depiction of gay life in the United States. Though *Queer as Folk* was criticized for not offering a diverse portrayal of the LGBT community and issues, its five seasons were groundbreaking in many ways.
- In 2001, HBO presents *Six Feet Under*, a gay-inclusive drama about a family running a funeral home in Los Angeles. Throughout the series' six seasons, youngest son David comes out to his family, dates and ultimately moves in with Keith Charles, and parents two sons. *Six Feet Under* is the recipient of three Golden Globes, nine Emmys, and three GLAAD Media Awards.
- In 2002, comedian Rosie O'Donnell came out in an interview with Diane Sawyer on ABC's *Primetime Thursday*.
- A few months later, in June, *The Wire*, a police drama, premiered on HBO and detective Shakima Greggs is a lesbian and becomes one of the central characters. *The Wire* is the recipient of a Peabody Award and was nominated for an Emmy, two GLAAD Media Awards, and 11 Image Awards.
- In 2003, Bravo introduced America to *Queer Eye for the Straight Guy*, which featured five openly gay hosts giving makeovers to straight men. It was a critic's hit and won several awards, including an Emmy for Outstanding Reality Program in 2004.
- Also in 2003, here!TV, America's first LGBT network, debuted as a premium cable channel and video on demand.

Ellen was on a roll, and nothing would stop her from her hosting duties on her successful daytime talk show—not even a back injury. When Ellen leaned over to pick up her dog in her kitchen in April 2008 and felt a tear, she knew it was bad, but she was already figuring out how to not miss a taping. She was confined to bed rest, so what would any dedicated comedian do? She added a hospital bed onto her set and conducted her talk show from it. Her guests were invited to sit in their own bed next to her. She jokingly told *American Idol* host Ryan Seacrest that "this is not a sweeps stunt or anything like that...not like what Regis Philbin did—that whole bypass surgery."[6]

In 2007, Ellen—who had already been the voice of an animated fish—became a character for American Greeting Cards. She inked a deal with American Greetings and designed a line of 32 cards.

Ellen shared her success with girlfriend Portia, whose career was going well, too. In 2003, Portia portrayed Lindsay on *Arrested Development*, a flamboyant and materialistic character who works on social causes, yet wants to be the center of attention. The character was married to Tobias, a psychiatrist and aspiring actor, but had homosexual overtones. She had also portrayed John F. Kennedy Jr.'s wife, Carolyn Bessette Kennedy, in a TBS made-for-TV movie *America's Prince*. She appeared in FX's medical drama *Nip/Tuck* as the character Julia McNamara's new girlfriend, Olivia Lord.

ANOTHER PUPPY EPISODE

"Now I feel completely comfortable with myself and I don't have to be fearful about something damaging my career if it gets out, because now I'm in control of it—sort of. No one can hurt me now."[7] No one could hurt Ellen now because she wouldn't let them, but it didn't mean that there wouldn't be more scandalous tabloid reports. She went from one fictional puppy episode in her fictional life to another almost exactly one decade later, but this time the real-life episode involved an actual puppy and a scandal that included death threats. Ellen eventually broke down into a puddle of tears on her talk show.

The saga started in 2007 when Ellen and Portia adopted a puppy named Iggy from Mutts and Moms, an animal rescue center in

California, in September 2007 for a $600 donation. The couple spent $3,000 having the diminutive dog neutered and trained, but unfortunately, the pooch didn't play well with the cats that already lived at Ellen's home. After hearing that her hairdresser wanted a pet, Ellen made the decision to give the cute canine to the family, believing that it would be going to a suitable home and that the rescue center would be pleased.

Regrettably, Ellen's attempt at generosity unwittingly violated the contract that she and Portia had signed with Mutts and Moms, and, in a drastic turn of events, the agency returned to reclaim the dog from the hairdresser's family. Ellen was devastated by this situation and the hurt that it caused the new adoptive family. It was difficult for Ellen to host her talk show and pretend that she was a happy, jovial person while this emotional scenario played out in her real life. One day smack in the middle of the off-camera chaos, Ellen—who typically begins her talk show with a menu of laughs and a dance—chose not to host her show her usual way and pretend that all was well in her life. Instead, she decided to be brutally honest and addressed her audience, telling them that she was sad and couldn't come out doing her regular performance. She proceeded to tell them exactly what had happened and how she was feeling.

She begged for the tiny pooch's return to what she thought was a capable family, but to no avail. Ellen apologized for her mistake and admitted her responsibility.

Unfortunately, the controversy was far from over when the show's filming ended that day. As a matter of fact, the situation took a nasty turn as the situation flared out of control over the next week. Media and gossip outlets went as far as nicknaming the whole situation "Poochgate," while others claimed that Ellen was in the "doghouse," and pictures of Ellen's weepy plea were plastered all over the Internet. Ellen ultimately cancelled two days of taping. The owners of the rescue center, Mutts and Moms, received threatening e-mails and phone calls. Mutts and Moms attorney Keith Fink played a tape for *Good Morning America* of what he called a legal threat, a voice mail message from a DeGeneres public relations representative telling the owners that Ellen's company was filing a legal case against the business and claiming they would take their side of the story to the media. As a result, Mutts and Moms stood firm in their decision to stick by their guidelines and chose not to return Iggy to the hairdresser's family.[8]

The country was once again at the water cooler and divided on an issue involving Ellen, and the media, tabloids, bloggers, writers, and news shows were obsessed with the story. Some were on the side of the family: "Wouldn't it make more sense for Mutts and Moms to give DeGeneres a little tap with a rolled up newspaper for breaking the rules but allow Iggy to stay with his new family? There was absolutely no reason for the group to make Iggy and the children suffer just to punish DeGeneres."[9]

Another thought on the subject, "I think that Ms. DeGeneres acted badly in not doing what was necessary to get Iggy and her cats to get along...And, if she were intent on getting rid of Iggy, I do not understand why she could not have first notified Mutts and Moms to facilitate the transfer to her hairdresser. On the other hand, I do not understand why Mutts and Moms reacted in an apparently peevish way and took Iggy from the hairdresser's family on some matter of principle."[10]

Some were on Ellen's side, including Richard Thompson, former Meow Mix owner, who now runs the animal-based Web site ZooToo.com. He came to Ellen's rescue, calling her a great rescue person. He has since teamed up with Ellen to improve rescue shelters.[11] Others weren't so nice calling Ellen a "blubbering idiot."[12] Some were even comical about the incident, suggesting that Ellen be admitted to a "drooling academy" for crying so much on television. Although it seemed like everyone who was anyone had a comment on the controversy, the Pew Research Center for the People and the Press proved that it was more water cooler talk than it was anything else. Their October 2007 study showed that the controversial meltdown really only generated a fair amount of news coverage. Overall, the public expressed relatively little interest in this story. Only 5 percent paid very close attention, and another 13 percent paid fairly close attention. Fully 59 percent said they were not following the story at all. However, most of the public says the DeGeneres story was overcovered by the media: 58 percent said it received too much coverage, 20 percent said it got the right amount of coverage, and 8 percent said it go too little coverage. Even those who were paying fairly close attention to the story overwhelmingly said it was overblown, according to the Center.

The public might not have paid attention, but *The Ellen DeGeneres Show* saw a bump in its ratings that week thanks to the publicity. The show's household rating jumped 5 percent that week, according to Nielsen Media Research, which marked a season high for the daytime talker.[13]

A WAR OF WORDS

But Ellen's difficulties with the media were far from over that year. Only one month later on November 5, 2007, Ellen's actions were targeted once again when the Writers Guild of America (WGA), which represents writers in the motion picture, broadcast, cable, and new media industries in both entertainment and news, called a strike of its East and West chapters to negotiate for a better contract.

While the strike did not affect the movie theater industry directly since movies are made a year or so before their release, it did have a serious impact on several talk shows, including the *Late Show with David Letterman*, *The Colbert Report*, and *The Ellen DeGeneres Show*, which are all produced daily.

Call it poor timing again, but while thousands of screenwriters on strike against film and TV studios rallied in New York and California, Ellen was scheduled to take her show on the road to the Big Apple. The New York wing of the WGA issued a statement saying DeGeneres—who is a member of both the WGA and the American Federation of Television and Radio Arts (AFTRA)—was not welcome in New York and threatened to picket her show if she went ahead with plans to tape there. She scrapped those plans.

Michael Winship, president of the East Coast branch of the WGA, said the organization was delighted with DeGeneres' decision to stay on the West Coast. "She knows that the Writers Guild East would have been there to protest her lack of solidarity, not only with her Guild writing staff but all the striking members of the Writers Guild, of which she is a member," Winship said in a statement.

"We find it sad that Ellen spent an entire week crying and fighting for a dog that she gave away, yet she couldn't even stand by writers for more than one day—writers who have helped make her extremely successful," the WGA East said.[14]

Ellen's production company, Telepictures Productions, issued a statement that said WGA strike rules exempted any writing by entertainers who performed the material themselves, which applied to Ellen. In addition, AFTRA, producers of *The Ellen DeGeneres Show*, and striking writers supported her decision, which Ellen made in order to prevent layoffs for the other nonwriting staff members. "I'm a host and have 135 staff members depending on me for a paycheck each week. I'm really just winging it," Ellen said. "I have to figure out how I'm going to walk out there and make people happy."[15]

On her first show during the strike, DeGeneres replaced her monologue and danced out to greet her audience instead. "We're in the middle of a strike....I love my writers. And in honor of them, I'm not going to do a monologue," she said, before dancing into the audience.[16] More than 12,000 writers joined the strike, which finally ended on February 12, 2008.

As private as Ellen was, the media loved to know what she was up to. From the time she orchestrated the most carefully planned coming out party in television, there was no turning back. The gossip columnists wanted to keep tabs on who she was dating, whether or not she would get pregnant with her partner or adopt a baby, what gay rights cause she would champion next, and, perhaps, what mistakes she would make. They documented her every move in a play-by-play during the writer's strike. She is a self-proclaimed nonpolitical person, but the gay community had hoped she would take a stand and use her talk show as a pulpit for more change. Everybody was watching and listening.

It took Ellen some time, but she began to see that her voice could make a difference. Ellen realized that people listened to what she said or did and that it was time to put that ability to use for the greater good. The fact was that Ellen was starting to command the same respect and recognition that Oprah Winfrey had earned in her career. Oprah is a philanthropist with an authoritative presence and someone who can dictate change by simply saying, "I like this book (or product or person)." So Ellen began to be much more vocal about topics that were near and dear to her heart, and, in turn, she became a catalyst for more change.

"NOW CHANGE THE MESSAGE"

I wish that I wasn't seen differently. I wish that people looked at me and just saw that I was a good person with a good heart. And that wants to make people laugh. And that's who I am. I also happen to be gay."

—*Ellen*

After her own coming out and the coming out of the fictional Ellen Morgan, Ellen DeGeneres said—even stressed—that she didn't want to be a role model for the gay community. However, slowly but surely Ellen has become a voice for those who need one. It might have started when she was devastated by the death of Matthew Shepard, a gay teen who was murdered on October 7, 1998. While the total number of anti-LGBT incidents reported to the National Coalition of Anti-Violence Programs fell 3 percent in 2006 from 1,440 to 1,393, these horrific incidents are still taking place.[17] While Ellen was fighting for the freedom to be who she was, other gays and lesbians were continuing to be murdered for being who they were.

In 2008, 15-year-old Lawrence "Larry" King was shot in the head at the E.O. Green School in Oxnard, California, by Brandon McInerney. Larry had asked Brandon to be his valentine. Brandon rejected Larry's offer and in anger took the young man's life. Ellen was distressed and turned her talk show stage into a metaphorical platform for peace and change. Ellen again addressed her audience teary eyed, but strong, and talked about this grisly crime and the need for change: "Larry is not a second-class citizen. I am not a second-class citizen. It is okay if you are gay. But I would like you to start paying attention to how often being gay is the punch line of a monologue. Or how often gay jokes are in a movie. And that kind of message—laughing at someone because they're gay—is just the beginning."[18]

On her Web site, Ellen provides several links to charitable organizations that can help those who are gay, lesbian, bisexual, transgender, and those who are questioning their sexuality. One of those Web sites is Remembering Lawrence (www.rememberinglawrence. org), which urges and keeps track of vigils in memory of Lawrence King, calling for an end to violence and harassment directed at LGBT people in schools.

A few days after Ellen poured her heart out, her girlfriend, Portia de Rossi, participated in a 60-second public service announcement (PSA). The PSA debuted on the gay TV network Logo in March 2008 and urged the end of hate violence. In addition to de Rossi, the 60-second announcement also featured Janet Jackson, Andre Benjamin, T. R. Knight, Taylor Swift, Sara Bareilles, and Calpernia Addams. The goal was that the PSA would spread the message in a positive light. According to GLAAD, in 2005, the University of Minnesota released three separate studies that concluded that exposure to positive depictions of gay television characters reduces prejudice. Polls have shown a shift in public opinion over the past decade about issues relating to gays and lesbians. A 1996 Pew Research poll found that 65 percent of respondents opposed same-sex marriage, versus 56 percent 10 years later. Also in 2006, Pew found that 48 percent of respondents opposed allowing gays to adopt, down from 57 percent in 1999.

PERSONAL CAUSES

In addition to spreading the word regarding Larry King, Ellen began to use her celebrity to lend her voice and her support to many other organizations that support the LGBT person, such as:

- The Trevor Project (http://www.thetrevorproject.org/home 2aspx), which operates the nation's only 24/7 crisis and suicide prevention helpline for gay, lesbian, bisexual, transgender, and questioning youths (866–4-U-TREVOR).
- The Gay and Lesbian Adolescent Social Services (GLASS), a private, nonprofit 501(c) (3) social service agency dedicated to providing a wide range of social and health care

services to children and youths who are in foster care, on probation, or who are homeless.

- PFLAG—Parents, Families and Friends of Lesbians and Gays—which promotes the health and well-being of LGBT persons and their families and friends through support, to cope with an adverse society; education, to enlighten an ill-informed public; and advocacy, to end discrimination and to secure equal civil rights. PFLAG provides opportunity for dialogue about sexual orientation and gender identity and acts to create a society that is healthy and respectful of human diversity.

- The Gay and Lesbian Alliance Against Defamation (GLAAD) (http://www.glaad.org/) is dedicated to promoting and ensuring fair, accurate, and inclusive representation of people and events in the media as a means of eliminating homophobia and discrimination based on gender identity and sexual orientation.

- GLSEN, or the Gay, Lesbian and Straight Education Network (http://www.glsen.org/splash/index.html), is the leading national education organization focused on ensuring safe schools for all students. Established nationally in 1995, GLSEN envisions a world in which every child learns to respect and accept all people, regardless of sexual orientation or gender identity/expression. More than 3,800 Gay-Straight Alliance student clubs nationwide have registered with GLSEN. GLSEN also sponsors the National Day of Silence on April 25, which, in 2008, was held in honor of Lawrence King.

Ellen has also become a spokesperson for victims of sexual abuse after she came forward and revealed that her stepfather had molested her when she was a teen caring for her sick mother. Ellen explained that she came out publicly years later because she wanted to save another child from going through the torment that she went through. Kathleen DeBold, the executive director of the Mautner Project, an organization that improves the health of lesbian, bisexual and transgender women who partner with women, and their families, through advocacy, education, research, and direct service, spoke out about DeGeneres' courage.

"Talking about abuse is often the first step to finding help and restoring a sense of well-being, and DeGeneres' openness about her traumatic experience at the hands of her stepfather will make that first step easier for thousands of women and girls," said DeBold. "By letting victims of sexual violence know they aren't alone and that it's okay to talk about what happened, DeGeneres has once again helped countless individuals of all genders and sexual orientations find the courage to tell their stories."[19]

On behalf of her mother, her friend Melissa Etheridge, and others, Ellen has also participated in spreading awareness of breast cancer detection, prevention, and fund-raising. Her mother, Betty, is a breast cancer survivor, and Ellen had her own scare with the disease after she discovered a growth in her breast a few years ago and had noncancerous tissue removed. Singer Melissa Etheridge was 43 years old and on her latest tour when she found a lump in her left breast that was malignant. She was treated for breast cancer with chemotherapy. Ellen has supported PinkTogether.com, an organization that generates awareness about breast cancer.

Ellen also hosted "Idol Gives Back," a charitable episode of the highly watched reality show *American Idol,* which raised more than $76 million in 2007 to benefit underprivileged children in America and overseas.

HI, IT'S ELLEN—THE GAY ONE

Ellen stresses that she never had the intention of getting involved in politics—especially in a public forum. But during the 2007–2008 season of *The Ellen DeGeneres Show,* she couldn't resist, especially after Oklahoma Republican Sally Kern addressed what she thought was a private group of Republicans with harsh words about lesbians and gays and their impact on society. In her speech, Kern stated that "the homosexual agenda is just destroying this nation" and that homosexuality poses a bigger threat to the United States than terrorism. "According to God's word, that is not the right kind of lifestyle," she said. "Studies show no society that has totally embraced homosexuality has lasted more than a few decades."

The recording sparked a public outcry after being shown on YouTube, and Kern received thousands of protest letters. Kern stood by her statements (although at one point, she tried to claim that they were taken out of context) and declared her First Amendment rights. During her show, Ellen made an attempt to phone Sally Kern and discuss "what societies have disappeared that I didn't know of." Kern didn't answer.

When she left a message, Ellen said, "Hi, it's Ellen DeGeneres, the gay one." Fox News said that Kern had no interest in talking to the entertainer. "That would be like throwing myself into the lion's den and I'm not going to do that," Kern said. Ellen had opened the doors for political discussions and had presidential candidates Hillary Rodham Clinton and Barack Obama on her show to discuss important topics including gay rights and, of course, to dance and bowl!

ELLEN VERSUS OPRAH

With the wildly phenomenal success of *The Ellen DeGeneres Show*, it was only a matter of time before the comparisons would begin between talk show host Ellen DeGeneres and daytime queen Oprah Winfrey. *The Oprah Winfrey Show* has been the highest rated talk show in the history of television. Oprah is also an Academy Award–nominated actress and a magazine publisher, and some consider her the most influential person in the world. Her show started on September 8, 1986, making it the longest-running daytime television talk show in the United States.

Since Oprah, daytime talk shows have come and gone, including those hosted by Megan Mullally, Rosie O'Donnell, Arsenio Hall, Ricki Lake, Tony Danza, Sharon Osbourne, and more. And although some have had longevity—including *Dr. Phil, Live with Regis and Kelly,* and *Rachael Ray*—others have not been able to compete with the media mogul. *Forbes* lists Oprah's media empire as a satellite radio show, magazine, Broadway musical (*The Color Purple*), and a stake in both Dr. Phil McGraw's talk show, *Dr. Phil,* and *Rachael Ray.*

While it seems that Oprah cannot be toppled from her media perch, Ellen has definitely made the perch crumble a bit as she competes head-to-head in many markets for viewers. In many cases, Ellen is leading Oprah in polls that compare popularity. In 2007,

Ellen appeared at the number eight spot of favorite television personalities, according to the Harris Poll. Oprah Winfrey held the top spot for the previous five years. But in January 2008, Ellen finally topped the Harris Poll list of favorite television personalities, ousting Winfrey. In a 2008 poll by AOL Television that gauges the popularity of different TV hosts, Ellen topped Oprah in several categories. Asked to choose which talk show host "made their day," 46 percent of the 1.35 million voters chose Ellen. Winfrey placed third, with 19 percent of the vote, 3 percentage points behind runner-up Regis Philbin.[20]

Media Life compares the two: "For sure, Winfrey is still way far out ahead in the ratings. Yet she's seen large declines this year. Season to date, she's averaging a 5.6 household rating, nearly a point ahead of No. 2 *Dr. Phil* but down 16 percent from the same time last year, according to Nielsen. All of the daytime talkers but DeGeneres are down from last year, most by double-digit percentages. But Winfrey has seen the steepest decline this season among women 18–49, where she slipped 23 percent."

This is an interesting result since Ellen went head-to-head in the big New York time slot against Oprah a few years ago. When Ellen's ratings in the big city began to fall, she asked to have her show moved to a different time slot because Oprah was pulling more than three times as many viewers as Ellen in New York. "I want our show to be funny and smart and it really bums me out that more people aren't seeing it," she says. She later joked, "I just wish she'd retire! She has enough money. She can go away. We all love her." But Oprah didn't go away, and a few years later, Ellen was ready to go head-to-head again and moved back to the prime 4 P.M.Oprah slot. Her show has been gaining ground since then.[21]

THE FUTURE

So, in January 2008, as Ellen DeGeneres addressed her studio and home audiences from her maroon chair on the set of her award-winning talk show, she asked for help rebuilding her devastated home state of Louisiana. And the Brad Pitt/Ellen DeGeneres Make It Right Web site is now a nominee for a Webby Award in the activism category. The Webbys are presented by the 550 members of the International Academy of Digital Arts and Sciences, which includes Internet coinventor Vinton Cerf, R/GA's Chief Bob Greenberg, *The Simpson's* creator Matt Groening, and movie-studio chief Harvey Weinstein. The Web community is given an opportunity to choose winners.

Ellen has come a long way since her humble beginnings as a small-town girl. Now a noted comedian, actress, and role model for the gay and straight communities, Ellen has overcome multiple forms of adversity—from being molested by her stepfather (who has since passed away) to coming out of the closet on national television and the accompanying backlash she took both personally and professionally. She briefly recoiled from show business and emerged again, rebuilding her career as a comedic icon who happens to be gay. Today, she stands as an award-winning, affluent Hollywood powerhouse, with *Forbes* magazine ranking her net worth at $65 million in 2007.

When asked why comedians do what they do, legendary talk show host and comedian Johnny Carson once said, "Everybody wants to be loved no matter what they do—even if you are a shoe clerk. Everybody wants to feel that somebody likes them, that they're accepted. By the fact that you find you can get laughs when you are in school and this is where most of the guys start, when they are growing up in the neighborhood—they're jerking around, doing silly things, interrupting the class. It's an attention-getting thing. I'm sure that's part of it to any performer—they *like* me, I'm accepted. I don't think that necessarily means or follows that all people who do comedy are hostile, bitter, unloved people striking back at society."[22]

Looking back, Ellen started in comedy because she wanted to make people laugh, but she also wanted what her brother, Vance, had when he began his music career—attention and prosperity. She has achieved that, but interestingly, now that she is at this point in her career, Ellen recognizes the ability to elicit change and awareness in many ways and the effect that giving back can have on others: "So I get to feel good because I'm making other people feel good. You know, I think initially everybody gets into showbiz in an egotistical way, like 'I want to be noticed and I want to be famous.' And then you recognize that that's not real and that's not what matters. What really does matter is that you're serving and what you're doing with your time here. And so it quickly changed for me from wanting to be famous to how can I make people happy and spread positivity—and try to not be a part of the rest of the negativity that's out there."[23]

Although going public and becoming a gay figurehead was not what Ellen had in mind when she came out in 1997, telling the world about her sexual orientation actually became a positive cata-lyst for change in her career, in the television industry, in her per-sonal life, and in the lives of others.

Legendary comedian Bob Newhart once said of Ellen, "That rev-elation could have ended her career, as she had to be aware, but she also knew she had to be honest. Thank God for Ellen DeGeneres. And it isn't often you see the name of a gay person and God in the same sentence these days."[24]

Today, Ellen blogs, vlogs (video blogs), and holds down her favor-ite job. To herself, she's just Ellen—not gay Ellen, or lesbian Ellen, or Ellen who came out of the closet, but just Ellen, and she'd like everyone else to think of her that way, too. She says, "No. I don't live my life like . . . I'm not even aware that I'm famous until people remind me. . . . And I don't think, I'm going home to my girlfriend and I'm gay. That's my life, that's who I love, my girlfriend and I are in love, but I don't think, I'm going home to my gay girlfriend. And I don't think, Oh, that's right, Elton's gay and I'm gay and we're together. To me, that is a problem, when there is too much emphasis. Also, it's not making steps forward. It's continuing to say 'us and them.' And I don't think it is 'us and them.'"[25]

I'M GETTING MARRIED!

You have to have funny faces and words, you can't just have words. It is a powerful thing, and I think that's why it's hard for people to imagine that women can do that, be that powerful.

—*Ellen*

On May 15, 2008, the California Supreme Court struck down the state's ban on same-sex marriage. The ruling declared that the state Constitution protects a fundamental "right to marry" that extends equally to same-sex couples. On August 16, 2008, Ellen married her girlfriend Portia de Rossi at their home in Beverly Hills, California. "It's something that we've wanted to do and we want it to be legal and we are very, very excited," said Ellen.[26]

NOTES

1. http://www.tvguide.com/News-Views/Interviews-Features/Article/default.aspx?posting=5AA22C63–7518–4759-BF36–6B28354B2CA3.

2. http://www.glaad.org/media/newspops_detail.php?id=3999.

3. http://64.233.169.104/search?q=cache:04pF-thQ3mEJ:www.gaymarketnews.com/2007/09/ellen-degeneres-gay-hero.html+%22elton+john%22+and+Ellen%27s+coming+out&hl=en&ct=clnk&cd=14&gl=us.

4. http://www.planetout.com/entertainment/news/?sernum=168.

5. http://www.glaad.org/media/resource_kit_detail.php?id=4000.

6. http://www.people.com/people/article/0,,20037295,00.html.

7. http://www.time.com/time/magazine/article/0,9171,986189,00.html.

8. http://abcnews.go.com/print?id=3739999.

9. http://freedomeden.blogspot.com/2007/10/ellen-degeneres-and-iggy-housebroken.html.

10. http://www.abolitionistapproach.com/?p=125.

11. http://www.foxnews.com/story/0,2933,316332,00.html.

12. http://theblemish.com/2007/10/ellen-degeneres-makes-children-cry/.

13. http://www.hollywoodreporter.com/hr/content_display/news/e3ic868cb7073298c93f6762c4c7d52dfec.

14. http://www.nzherald.co.nz/section/1501119/story.cfm?c_id=1501119&objectid=10475472.

15. http://www.dailynews.com/ci_7399722.

16. http://www.javno.com/en/bestseller/clanak.php?id=97059.

17. http://64.233.169.104/search?q=cache:xVVYRPth-8kJ:www.ncavp.org/common/document_files/Reports/2006NtnlHVReportExecSumm.pdf+National+Coalition+of+Anti-Violence+Programs+fell+3+percent+in+2006&hl=en&ct=clnk&cd=1&gl=us.

18. http://www.planetout.com/entertainment/news/?sernum=168.

19. http://www.pridesource.com/article.shtml?article=14477.

20. http://www.medialifemagazine.com/artman2/publish/Dayparts_update_51/Oprah_s_the_queen_but_Ellen_s_the_fave.asp.

21. http://www.nypost.com/seven/11082006/tv/get_me_out_of_here__tv_michael_starr.htm.

22. Larry Wilde, *Great Comedians Talk about Comedy* (Mechanicsburg, PA: Executive Books, 2000), p. 171.

23. First for Women, April 7, 2008, p. 43.

24. http://www.time.com/time/magazine/article/0,9171,1187186,00.html?iid=chix-sphere.

25. http://findarticles.com/p/articles/mi_m1589/is_2005_Jan_18/ai_n9483867/print.

26. http://www.usmagazine.com/Ellen-DeGeneres-Portia-De-Rossi-to-Say-I-Do.

Appendix

AWARDS

1991   American Comedy Awards: Named "Best Female Stand-Up."

1995   Screen Actors Guild Award: Nominated Actor Outstanding Performance by a Female Actor in a Comedy Series for *Ellen*.
Won People's Choice Award Favorite Female Performer in a New TV Series.
Primetime Emmy: Outstanding Lead Actress in a Comedy Series for *Ellen*. Won American Comedy Award Funniest Female Performer in a TV Special (Leading or Supporting) Network, Cable, or Syndication for the *46th Annual Primetime Emmy Awards*.

1996   Nominated Golden Globe Best Performance by an Actress in a TV Series—Comedy/Musical for *Ellen*.
Nominated American Comedy Award Funniest Female Performer in a TV Series (Leading Role) Network, Cable, or Syndication for *Ellen*.
Nominated Emmy Outstanding Individual Performance in a Variety or Music Program for the *38th Annual Grammy Awards* for hosting the show.

1997   Screen Actors Guild Award: Nominated Actor Outstanding Performance by a Female Actor in a Comedy Series for *Ellen*.

Won Primetime Emmy: Outstanding Writing in a Comedy Series.

Won Peabody Award for *Ellen*.

Won GLAAD Media Award for Outstanding TV Comedy Series.

Named Entertainment Weekly "Entertainer of the Year."

Won Emmy Outstanding Writing for a Comedy Series for *Ellen*, shared (1994).

Nominated Emmy Outstanding Guest Actress in a Comedy Series for *The Larry Sanders Show*.

Nominated Emmy Outstanding Lead Actress in a Comedy Series for *Ellen*.

1998   Won Stephen F. Kolzak Award from the 9th Annual GLAAD Media Awards—presented to an openly LGBT media professional who has made a significant difference in promoting equal rights for the community.

Nominated for Writers Guild of America, for *Ellen*.

Viewers for Quality Television Award: Nominated for Best Actress in a Quality Comedy Series, *Ellen*.

Golden Satellite Award: Nominated for Award Best Performance by an Actress in a Television Series—Comedy or Musical for *Ellen*.

Nominated Golden Globe Best Performance by an Actress in a TV Series—Comedy/Musical for *Ellen*.

Nominated Emmy Outstanding Lead Actress in a Comedy Series for *Ellen*.

1999   Golden Satellite Award: Won for Best Performance by an Actress in a Television Series—Comedy or Musical for *Ellen*.

American Comedy Award: Nominated Funniest Female Guest Appearance in a TV Series for *The Larry Sanders Show*.

American Comedy Award: Nominated Funniest Female Performer in a TV Series (Leading Role) Network, Cable, or Syndication for *Ellen*.

American Comedy Award: Won Funniest Female Performer in a TV Special (Leading or Supporting) Network, Cable, or Syndication for *1998 VH1 Fashion Awards*.

2000   Nominated Emmy Outstanding Made for Television Movie for *If These Walls Could Talk 2* (2000) (TV), shared with executive producers.

2001   Nominated Emmy Outstanding Individual Performance in a Variety or Music Program for *Ellen DeGeneres: The Beginning.*

Nominated Emmy Outstanding Variety, Music, or Comedy Special for *Ellen DeGeneres: The Beginning,* shared with executive producer.

American Comedy Award: Won Funniest Female Performer in a TV Special (Leading or Supporting) Network, Cable, or Syndication for *Ellen DeGeneres: The Beginning.*

2004   Daytime Emmy: Won Outstanding Talk Show for *The Ellen DeGeneres Show.*

Saturn Award: Won Best Supporting Actress for Finding Nemo (2003).

Kids Choice Awards: Won Favorite Voice from an Animated Movie for *Finding Nemo.*

Nominated MTV Movie Award Best Comedic Performance for *Finding Nemo.*

Nominated Emmy Outstanding Individual Performance in a Variety or Music Program for *Ellen DeGeneres: Here and Now.*

Outstanding Variety, Music, or Comedy Special for *Ellen DeGeneres: Here and Now* shared with executive producer.

2005   Daytime Emmy: Won Outstanding Talk Show for *The Ellen DeGeneres Show.*

Daytime Emmy: Won Outstanding Talk Show Host for *The Ellen DeGeneres Show.*

Daytime Emmy: Won Outstanding Special Class Writing for *The Ellen DeGeneres Show.*

People's Choice Awards: Won Favorite Daytime Talk Show Host.

People's Choice Awards: Won Favorite Funny Female Star.

2006   Daytime Emmy: Won Outstanding Talk Show for *The Ellen DeGeneres Show.*

Daytime Emmy: Won Outstanding Talk Show Host for *The Ellen DeGeneres Show.*

Daytime Emmy: Won Outstanding Special Class Writing for *The Ellen DeGeneres Show*.

People's Choice Awards: Won Favorite Daytime Talk Show Host.

People's Choice Awards: Won Favorite Funny Female Star.

2007   Daytime Emmy Award: Won Outstanding Talk Show Host for *The Ellen DeGeneres Show*.

Chosen as one of *People* magazine's annual 100 most beautiful people in the world.

TV Land Award: Nominated TV Moment That Became Headline News for "The Puppy Episode," *Ellen*.

Nominated Emmy Outstanding Individual Performance in a Variety or Music Program for the *79th Annual Academy Awards*.

2008   People's Choice Award: Won Favorite Funny Female Star, Favorite Talk Show Host.

BIBLIOGRAPHY

Ajaye, Franklyn. *Comic Insights: The Art of Stand-up Comedy*. Los Angeles: Silman-James Press, 2002.

Alter, Jonathan. "Gore's Gay Gambit." *Newsweek*, October 27, 1997.

Atkin, Hillary. "From Hopeful to Household Name Success as Standup, Sitcom Star, Awards Host Prepared Her for Talk Show." *TelevisionWeek*, January 2008.

Brooks, Tim. *The Complete Directory of Primetime Network and Cable TV Shows, 1946 to Present*. New York: Ballantine Books, 2003.

Carter, Bill. "At Lunch With: Ellen DeGeneres; Dialed God (Pause). He Laughed." *New York Times*, April 13, 1994.

DeGeneres, Betty. *Love, Ellen: A Mother/Daughter Journey*. New York: William Morrow & Co., 1999.

DeGeneres, Ellen. *My Point and I Do Have One*. New York: Bantam, 1995.

Della Casa, Brenda. "Vance DeGeneres Knows Everything." The Phat Free., May 27, 2006, http://www.thephatfree.com.

Fitzgerald, Toni. "Oprah's the Queen, but Ellen's the Fave." *Media Life*, March 27, 2008.

Foley, Bridget. "Ellen." *W Magazine*, March 2007.

Gallagher, John. "Divine Cancellation—ABC-TV Cancels 'Ellen'— Battling the Religious Right: Lose One." *The Advocate*, June 9, 1998.

Gallagher, John. "Ellen DeGeneres: 'We're Not Coming Back.'" *The Advocate*, April 14, 1998.

Gay, Verne. "All About Ellen." *Newsday,* April 24, 1997.

Goodman, Walter. "Critic's Notebook; Commercial TV Gets Commercial Threats." *New York Times,* April 24, 1989.

Gutterman, Dawn Wolfe. "Ellen DeGeneres Comes Out as a Sex Abuse Survivor." PrideSource.com, June 2, 2005.

Handy, Bruce. "He Called Me Ellen DeGenerate?" *Time,* April 1997.

Heche, Anne. *Call Me Crazy.* New York: Washington Square Press, 2003.

Jacobs, A. J. "Out." *EW* Online, http://www.ew.com/ew/article/ 0,,294355,00.html.

James, Caryn. "Critic's Notebook: All Right, Goodbye Already!; Parting Is Such Sweet Sitcom." *New York Times,* May 12, 1998.

Johnson, Ian. "Ellen DeGeneres: Gay Hero." *Gay Market News,* September 12, 2007.

Kaufman, Debra. "DeGeneres Proved She Was Right Choice as Host of Troubled Post-9/11 Emmy Telecast." *Television Week* Online.

Kaufman, Gil. "Johnny Carson, 'King of Late-Night TV,' Dies at Age 79." MTV.com, January 24, 2005, http://www.mtv.com/news/ articles/1496154/20050124/index.jhtml?headlines=true.

Kort, Michele. "Portia Heart & Soul." *The Advocate,* September 13, 2005.

LaSalle, Mick. "Little Right About 'Mr. Wrong.'" *San Francisco Chronicle,* February 17, 1996, p. B-1.

Lehner, Marla. "Ellen DeGeneres: I Was Molested." *People,* May 18, 2005.

Levine, Hallie. "Mom Shares Ellen's Joy—New Gal Pal Eases Pain of Heche Split." *New York Post,* October 24, 2000.

Marin, Rick, and Sue Miller. "Ellen Steps Out; Here Comes TV's First Leading Lesbian." *Newsweek,* April 14, 1997.

McMahon, Ed. *Here's Johnny!: My Memories of Johnny Carson, The Tonight Show, and 46 Years of Friendship.* New York: Berkley, 2006.

Nudd, Tim. "Ellen DeGeneres: Portia Is 'My Perfect Fit.'" *People* Online, January 7, 2007, http://www.people.com/people/ article/0,,20009962,00.html.

Peiffer, Kim. "Ellen DeGeneres Hosting Shows from Hospital Bed." *People* Online, April 30, 2007, http://www.people.com/ people/article/0,,20037295,00.html.

Phillips, Stone. "Catching Up with Ellen DeGeneres." MSNBC.com, November 8, 2004, http://www.msnbc.msn.com/id/6430100/.

Reed, Jennifer. *Queer Popular Culture: Literature, Media, Film and Television*. Houndmills Palgrave Macmillan, 2007.

Reuters. "Ellen DeGeneres Targeted as Pressure Mounts in Hollywood Writers' Strike." *New Zealand Herald*, November 12, 2007.

Rose, Chris. "Melancholy Ellen." *Times-Picayune*, Living section, pg. 1, February 11, 2003.

Schwarzbaum, Lisa. "Shtick in the Mud." *EW Online*, September 8, 2005, http://www.ew.com/ew/article/0,,298566,00.html.

Shister, Gail. "Intimate Portrait." *The Record*, February 2, 2000, p. Y1.

Shister, Gail. "Up with People." *Pittsburgh Post Gazette*, March 13, 1998, Arts & Entertainment, pg. 40.

Silverman, Stephen M. "Ellen DeGeneres Helped Mom with Cancer Fight." *People*, September 2007, http://www.people.com/people/article/0,,20058779, 00.html.

Snierson, Dan. "Hostess Treat." *EW Online*, February 2, 2007, http://www.ew.com/ew/article/0,,20007870_20007899_20009762_,00.html.

Stockwell, Anne. "A Day in the Year of Ellen." *The Advocate*, January 18, 2005.

Tracy, Kathleen. *Ellen: The Real Story of Ellen DeGeneres*. New York: Pinnacle Books, 2005.

Tucker, Ken. "Jerry-Rigged." *EW Online*, March 25, 1994.

Vilanch, Bruce. "The Happy Couple—Lesbian Pair Ellen DeGeneres and Anne Heche." *The Advocate*, June, 24, 1997.

Weber, Bruce. "Comedy Review; As Insecure as the Fans, but Funnier." *New York Times*, June 21, 2002, http://query.nytimes.com/gst/fullpage.html?res=980CE0DF123FF932A15755C0A9649C8B63&sec=&spon=&pagewanted=2.

Wieder, July. "Ellen: Born Again—Ellen DeGeneres Interview." *The Advocate*, March 14, 2000.

Wilde, Larry. *Great Comedians Talk about Comedy*. Mechanicsburg, PA: Executive Books, 2000.

Zabel, Bryce. "Ellen Confirms 'Yep, I'm Gay.'" *Time*, April 14, 1997.

Zonkel, Phillip. "The Regeneration of Ellen DeGeneres." *Press-Telegram*, June 21, 2000, Lifestyle Section, pg. 1.

Zwecker, Bill. "Ex Might Sue Ellen—and the Sitcom Star She's With." *Chicago Sun-Times*, January 11, 2005, Features, p. 36.

INDEX

American Express, 70
Anatomy of a Hate Crime, 55
Atlanta, Texas, 6
Awards: American
    Comedy Award, 26, 29;
    CableACE, 26

Bono, Chastity, 51, 52
Breast cancer, 2, 7

Caroline's, 18
Carrey, Jim, 5
Carson, Johnny, 16, 21,
    22, 25. *See also The
    Tonight Show*
Charity, 86
Christian Scientists, 4, 5
Coming out: backlash,
    37–41; Ellen Morgan,
    35; "Yep, I'm
    Gay," 43
Coneheads, 26
Congress, 55
The Cosby Show, 27

DeGeneres, Betty, 2, 6, 7, 20,
    44–45, 47, 60
DeGeneres, Elliott, 2, 15
DeGeneres, Vance, 2, 4, 6, 13, 18,
    19, 40, 73
Dern, Laura, 40, 78
De Rossi, Portia, 66–70, 79; and
    Francesca Gregorini, 68; and
    mariage to Ellen, 92
Divorce, 4, 5
Doctor Doolittle, 54

EdTV, 55
Ellen, 30–31, 33–41
Ellen DeGeneres Show, The, 65, 70
The Ellen Show, 61, 63
Emmy, 45, 61, 63
Etheridge, Melissa, 88
Everybody Loves Raymond, 27

Finding Nemo, 64
The Four Agreements, 60
Friends, 26, 39
The Funny Thing Is . . ., 66

Gay and Lesbian Adolescent
    Social Services (GLASS), 86
Gay and Lesbian Alliance Against
    Defamation (GLAAD), 14, 37,
    40, 41, 45, 52, 54, 77, 87
Gay, Lesbian and Straight
    Education Network
    (GLSEN), 87
Gays: Rights, 13: Stonewall riots,
    13, 14; Gay marriage, 92
Goodbye Lover, 55
Gore, Al, 46, 47
Grammy, 73

HBO, 17, 25; Command
    Performance: One Night
    Stand, 26; Ellen DeGeneres:
    The Beginning 61; Here
    & Now—Modern Life 64;
    Women of the Night, 26; Young
    Comedians Reunion, 25
Heath, Ben, 6
Heche, Anne, 45, 48, 54, 56
Hedison, Alexandra, 59, 60, 66, 70
Home Improvement, 27
Human Rights Campaign
    (HRC), 47
Hurricane Katrina, 1, 2, 72, 90

If These Walls Could Talk, 56
Iggy, 80–82
Improv, 18, 21; Laugh Factory, 18

The Jeff Foxworthy Show, 27

Kern, Sally, 88, 89
King, Larry (Lawrence), 85

The Laramie Project, 55
Laurie Hill, 26
Lesbian, 11, 12, 43

Love, Ellen: A Mother/Daughter
    Journey (biography), 2, 14

Make It Right NOLA
    Foundation, 2
The Matthew Shepard Story, 55
Mautner Project, 87
McMahon, Ed, 21
Metairie, Louisiana, 5
Miguel Ruiz, Don, 60, 61
Molestation, 8
Morgan, Ellen, 27–30
Mr. Wrong, 32
My Point and I Do Have One . . . ,
    31, 32

New Orleans, 1, 3, 17; University
    of, 11

Ochsner Foundation Hospital, 2
Open House, 25

Paparazzi, 33
Parents, Families & Friends of
    Lesbians and Gays (PFLAG),
    47, 87
Pass Christian, Mississippi, 2, 12
Perkoff, Kat, 16
Pertain, Ricky, 11
"Phone Call to God" sketch, 16, 22
Pitt, Brad, 1, 90
"The Puppy Episode," 33–41, 45, 78

Queer as Folk, 79
Queer Eye for the Straight Guy, 78

Rock, Chris, 5
Roseanne, 27, 39

Sawyer, Diane, 4, 13
Seinfeld, 27

September 11th, 62
79th Annual Academy Awards,
    71, 72
Shepard, Matthew, 54; *Anatomy
    of a Hate Crime*, 55; *The
    Laramie Project*, 55
Showtime, 17, 18
Six Feet Under, 79
Soap, 38

These Friends of Mine, 27–30
    (*See also Ellen*)

Time, 43
*Tonight Show Starring
    Johnny Carson,
    The*, 16, 21, 22,
    25
The Trevor Project, 86

Will & Grace, 53
Winfrey, Oprah, 89
Writer's strike, 83, 84

Young Comedians Reunion, 25

About the Author

LISA IANNUCCI is an independent scholar.